Four Strange Books

of the Bible

Four Strange Books
of the Bible

JONAH / DANIEL / KOHELETH / ESTHER

Elias Bickerman

SCHOCKEN BOOKS · NEW YORK

First published by Schocken Books 1967
10 9 8 7 6 5 4 3 2   85 86 87 88

Library of Congress Cataloging in Publication Data
Bickerman, E. J. (Elias Joseph), 1897–
    Four strange books of the Bible.
    Includes bibliographies.
    1. Bible. O.T. Jonah—Criticism, interpretation,
etc. 2. Bible. O.T. Daniel—Criticism, interpretation,
etc. 3. Bible. O.T. Ecclesiastes—Criticism, interpretation, etc. 4. Bible. O.T. Esther—Criticism,
interpretation, etc.   I. Title.
BS1200.B5   1984   221   84-22199

Manufactured in the United States of America
ISBN 0–8052–0774–0

Preface

As a classical scholar the author is interested in the books of the Bible which were written in the age of Greek intellectual dominance. In the present work he tries to understand Jonah, Daniel, Koheleth, and Esther as witnesses to the mentality of men of that period in the ancient Near East.

His learned friends, Boaz Cohen of the Jewish Theological Seminary, Judah Goldin of Yale, and Gerson D. Cohen and Morton Smith of Columbia University, helped with information, advice, and criticism. He is under particular obligation to H. L. Ginsberg of the Jewish Theological Seminary, who allowed him to use a still unpublished translation of Ecclesiastes, and on whose interpretation the chapter on Koheleth depends (see his paper in *Vetus Testamentum*, 1954). The pages on Daniel and Koheleth, differently organized and annotated, will appear in the forthcoming *History of the Jews in the Greek Age*. Louis Finkelstein, Chancellor of the Jewish Theological Seminary, has generously permitted the use of this material here. The pages on the Greek Esther are reprinted from *Proceedings of the American Academy of Jewish Research*, V, 20 (1954), with permission of Abraham Halkin of the Academy. Much of the material in the chapter on Jonah appeared in French in *Revue d'Histoire et de Philosophie Religieuses*, 1965. The editorial help of Oscar Shaftel, of Schocken Books, is also acknowledged; and I shall not forget that the late T. Herzl Rome encouraged the writing of this book and accepted it for publication.

Columbia University   ELIAS BICKERMAN
June 1967

Contents

List of Illustrations

JONAH
or
THE
UNFULFILLED
PROPHECY

Jonah and the Whale

THE Book of Jonah contains only forty-eight verses according to the reckoning of the ancient Hebrew scribes. But the name of no prophet is better known to the man in the street. Jonah is that man who was swallowed alive by a whale and was spewed up three days later, unhurt. The Hebrew Bible contains fifteen prophetic books, but Mahomet speaks only of Jonah, "him of the fish." As early as the second century B.C.E. Jonah in the belly of the sea monster and Daniel among the lions appeared as outstanding examples of deliverance, and in the eyes of the first Christians the emergence of Jonah alive from the depths of the sea prefigured the Resurrection.

The miracle which awed the faithful also tickled the fancy of unbelievers. Celsus, who in the second century wrote a refutation of Christianity, suggested that the Christians should worship not Jesus but Jonah or Daniel, whose miracles outdo the Resurrection. Three centuries later, Jerome and Augustine tell us, Jonah was still a matter of jest to heathen scoffers, and even believers found it incredible, particularly if they had a Greek education, that a man could have stayed alive three days in the belly of a whale. Learned Christians, embarrassed, appealed to no less wondrous Greek myths, as of Zeus transformed into a swan to seduce Leda: "You believe in those tales and say that to the Deity all things are possible." Augustine rebuts the skeptics with the argument that all miracles are by definition impossible.

In modern times exegetes have often tried to vindi-

cate the episode by quoting sailor yarns. Two years after
the publication of Darwin's *On the Origin of Species*
Canon Pusey collected some such old salt's tales in his
commentary on Jonah (1861). Other pious writers had
recourse to a rationalist explanation of the miracle: Jonah
was picked up by a ship named "Big Fish," or he spent
three nights in an inn "At the Sign of the Whale," or in
a bathing establishment called "The Whale." A more ac-
ceptable rationalist guess was that Jonah had dreamed
the whole incident when, during the storm, he fell into
a profound sleep (Jonah 1:5).[1]

Despite the discomfort the story arouses in the faithful, its literal historicity was declared as late as 1956 in a
Catholic encyclopedia, and admitted, albeit halfheartedly,
in a Protestant biblical dictionary in 1962. In a mosque
bearing the name of Jonah near the oil derricks of Mosul
the pious visitor can still admire the remains of Jonah's
whale.

One thing is certain: the Book of Jonah is an ab-
sorbing short story that has commanded attention for
some twenty-five centuries. Its plot is simple: a prophet
announces the destruction of a city; the inhabitants repent and are spared. This sermonizing theme is transformed into an exciting tale by holding back the solution
and keeping the reader in suspense.

From the Jonah Fresco in the Catacomb of Callistus, Rome (generally dated as of the third century). The "big fish" is here depicted as the legendary "hippocampus."

Part of a mosaic (fourth century), depicting the story of Jonah, in the Christian Basilica at Aquileia, Italy.

From the Aquileia mosaic. Jonah's ejection by the sea beast. Note, at the upper right, part of the next "panel" in the adventures of Jonah: the mosaic version of the gourd trellis.

From the same mosaic. Jonah resting "on the east side of Nineveh," shaded by the gourd trellis, still surrounded by marine life.

The Unwilling Prophet

The story of Jonah has a cast of three characters: God, the sinful people of Nineveh, and the prophet. The Deity is outside of time and place. The Ninevites might be the source of dramatic suspense in easily imaginable variations of the plot. But the biblical book is about Jonah.

The word of the Lord came to Jonah to go to Nineveh and to "proclaim against it." A prophet is God's crier announcing the divine will, but a messenger may be unwilling to transmit the message. The Jewish commentator Ibn Ezra, in the twelfth century, cited the case of Moses who was reluctant to accept the call from the Lord (Exod. 4:10). The motif of man failing to heed a divine call appears often in history and in fiction. Cicero, for instance, in his work on divination tells of a peasant who in a dream received an order from Jupiter to convey to the Romans the displeasure of the supreme god. The man lingered, and his son died. The call was repeated in a new dream. The man still hesitated and fell paralyzed. At last, carried on a stretcher, he transmitted the divine message and, healed immediately, was able to walk home.

Centuries before Cicero the Babylonian seers, contemporaries of Jonah, swore to reveal signs and portents to the king. "If you do not speak, you shall die." An Assyrian seer tells us that was what happened to his mother. She neglected to transmit a divine message directly to the king, but entrusted it to a careless courtier. The revelation did not reach the king, and she died. In terms of modern psychology a man who believes he has received a divine call and is slow to follow it becomes a victim of his own inadequacy. James Nayler, a former officer of Cromwell, heard a voice ordering him to leave his house. But, as he relates, "not being obedient in going forth, the wrath of God was upon me." He fell sick, "and none thought I would have lived." At last, made willing, he left home suddenly without taking leave of his family. "I was commanded to go to the West."

In our days a hereditary seer in former French Guinea, when his father died, refused to exercise the ancestral calling, and fled abroad. But visions tormented him and he had to return to his village and accept his task. In Greek poetry this need to utter the prophetic message is exemplified in Cassandra, who could not stop foretelling the coming woes of Troy, though her words were not believed.

The author of the Book of Jonah used the theme of the disobedient prophet to build up the first suspense in his tale. Jonah was bidden to go eastward to Nineveh, a city near the site of modern Mosul, in Iraq. But Jonah boarded a ship at Jaffa to flee to Tarshish, in the far west. How would he be compelled to fulfill the command? In such cases the usual means of celestial discipline was bodily pain. But this trite motif is shunned by our author.

A great tempest strikes Jonah's ship. According to the ideas of the ancients the ship must therefore be carrying an enemy of the gods. In fifth-century Athens, Antiphon, a contemporary of Socrates, could argue before the popular court that his client, being prosecuted for murder, must be innocent because the ship on which he traveled had arrived safely. When Diagoras, surnamed the Atheist, made a sea voyage, a storm broke out. But the philosopher pointed to other ships in distress and asked whether Diagoras was aboard those ships too. To dispose of this ironical argument Theodore of Mopsuestia, a learned Christian commentator of the fourth century, assured his readers that the tempest struck Jonah's ship only.

The drawing of lots directs the mariners' attention to Jonah, and the prophet owns his guilt, that he was fleeing "from the presence of the Lord." He adds that because of him the great tempest endangers the ship. "Take me up, and cast me forth into the sea." Unwillingly, the sailors throw him into the sea, "and the sea ceased from its raging." The narrator here adapts a motif that occurs in folk tales from Iceland to Korea: a man is thrown overboard to placate the hostile element.

Jonah's self-sacrifice shows his faith in God's justice; thus the reader knows in advance that the prophet will be saved. But how? Commenting on Ecclesiastes' surprising advice, "Cast thy bread upon the waters," the rabbis collected many stories about righteous men who went down with ships but were carried safe ashore by waves. The author of Jonah, however, delays the happy ending by introducing a new danger: Jonah was swallowed by "the great fish," which, in medieval imagination, became a whale. After three days he was spewed out by the monster.

The Church fathers, commenting on "the great fish," cited for the benefit of unbelievers a Greek myth as a parallel to the experience of Jonah. When Herakles fought a sea monster to save the Trojan princess Hesione, he was swallowed and he overcame the enemy by hacking away at its entrails. Modern commentators add further parallels from fairy tales. But Jonah did not fight the whale. He was saved by it from drowning. In legend, animals often save the innocent victim. The Greek poet Arion (c. 625 B.C.E.) jumped into the sea to save his life from greedy seamen. A dolphin carried him on its back to land. The shipwrecked Herakles, like Jonah, was swallowed by a sea monster and thus saved from death in the sea. So the episode of the whale, in folklore classification, fits under the heading of animal helpers.

Theodore of Mopsuestia and other ancient readers asked whether there was no more conventional way of saving Jonah. But Jerome, no mean stylist himself, appreciated the literary effect of surprise: "You will note that where you would think should be the end of Jonah, there was his safety."

The narrator, however, believes in the historicity of the accident. In the belly of the fish Jonah utters a psalm which, as Jerome noted, is not a prayer for rescue, but a thanksgiving for grace already granted. This anomaly disturbed the ancient Greek translator and caused him to change the past tenses of the original. Jews who read the original Hebrew text concluded that the psalm was spoken by Jonah after being spewed out on shore: the Jewish historian Flavius Josephus toward the end of the first century knows and accepts this interpretation. A generation before Josephus, the Jewish moralist Philo of Alexandria had retold the story of Jonah in Greek, substituting for the psalm a more appropriate supplication. In medieval Hebrew paraphrase (in *Pirke Rabbi Eliezer*), Jonah prays to be restored to life.

The incongruity between the psalm and its context indicates that the narrator must have used a psalm already circulating under the name of Jonah. For him as for his hero and for religious men of every faith, it was unthinkable that a man could fail to pray in mortal danger, and be saved without supplication. As Mahomet explained, had Jonah not praised God he would have remained in the whale's belly till the resurrection of the dead. The honest narrator could not and dared not invent the instrument of salvation. The prayer with which Jonah appeals to God—"Thou didst cast me into the depth, in the heart of the seas . . ."—was in the eyes of the narrator related to the episode of "the great fish." Perhaps, like Jerome later, he believed that in the depth of the sea Jonah, being a prophet, could see himself offering thanks to God in the Temple. The function of the episode in the plot is, however, clear: God, says the Church father Irenaeus, allowed Jonah to be swallowed and vomited forth by the sea monster so that he might be subdued to God's will.

Jonah in Nineveh

As we have seen, the official teaching of the Synagogue was not unique, that a man who suppresses a divine oracle is condemned to death by heaven; and Jonah son of Amittai was cited as the warning example. Miraculously saved from death, Jonah learned his lesson. Again bidden to go to Nineveh, he obeyed and delivered the oracle. The reader would now expect to be told of fire and brimstone falling upon the new Sodom. But the narrator introduces a new reversal of situation. Unlike the inhabitants of Sodom, among whom not even ten righteous men could be found (Gen. 18:32), the Ninevites repent and are spared by God.

The reader might assume that the prophet would be happy at the outcome of his mission. Lo, he is displeased exceedingly: "It is better for me to die than to live." But God neither heeds this arrogance nor punishes the presumptuous servant. Rather, he creates a climbing plant to shelter Jonah from the sun. But the next morning the gourd perishes. When Jonah complains, he receives the answer: You are concerned about a gourd, should I not be concerned about Nineveh, "wherein are more than sixscore thousand persons that cannot discern between their right hand and their left hand, and also much cattle?" This argument by analogy is rather weak. Jonah was pained not by the withering of a plant but by the loss of the shelter.

The story, at any rate, ends here and we are left to believe that the Lord's rebuke convinced Jonah of his second error just as the episode of the sea monster had shown him the uselessness of his flight. So two extraordinary miracles, material arguments in the dialogue between God and His prophet, are the hinges on which the whole narrative turns. Ancient readers understood the composition of the book. On Christian sarcophagi the story of Jonah is represented in two tableaux: left, the sea dragon which first gulps and then disgorges Jonah; right, Jonah reclining under the gourd.

Jonah as Friend of Israel

The narrative structure of the book, however, cannot explain the psychological problem of its hero. An occasional messenger of revelation, such as the Roman farmer mentioned above, may doubt the authenticity of his mission or his capacity to fulfill it. But Jonah son of Amittai, from Gath-hepher in Galilee, who lived in the reign of Jeroboam II, that is, in the middle of the eighth century B.C.E., is named in the Second Book of Kings (14:25) as the *nabi* (prophet) who foretold the territorial expansion of Israel from the region of Hamath to the Dead Sea. How could he, "a servant of YHWH, the God of Israel," believe that he could escape from the Lord? "The lion roared, who will not fear? The Lord God has spoken, who can but prophesy?" (Amos 3:8). And why should he be pained to death at the display of divine mercy? Ephraem, in his homily on the Repentance of Nineveh, makes the spared Ninevites say to Jonah: "What would it have profited you if we had perished? You became famous by our repentance."

The traditional Jewish explanation was that Jonah, being a prophet, knew in advance that Nineveh would repent and be saved. But that would put to shame stiff-necked Israel. "Since the heathen are nearer to repentance, I might be causing Israel to be condemned." The prophet knew, says Jerome, that "the repentance of the Gentiles would be the downfall of the Jews."

This interpretation of Jonah's motives became popular after the destruction of Jerusalem and the Temple in 70 C.E. and the failure of the great rebellion of Bar Kochba against Rome in 135 C.E. The Jews understood that God alone could redeem Israel, but they also knew that their transgressions, from the violation of the Sabbath to internecine hatred, prevented their claims and complaints from reaching the heavenly throne. Reinterpreting Scripture in terms of their own needs and hopes, the pious now believed that the patriarchs and the prophets of yore were advocates of Israel before God, offering their lives to atone for Israel. Simeon ben Azzai, a contemporary of Rabbi Akiba, asserted that God spoke to the prophets (and they prophesied) only because of the merits of Israel. Seen from this point of view, Jonah's

mission does not make sense. Nineveh was the capital of
the Assyrians, which, like Rome in the days of the rabbis,
imposed its yoke upon the Holy Land and the holy people. Nahum, whose words have been preserved in the
same prophetic scroll as the story of Jonah, exulted at
the destruction of Nineveh, "the bloody city . . . full
of lies and rapine" (Nah. 3:1).

Perplexed, some Jewish commentators thought that
the Ninevites had been spared because of the merits of
their ancestor Asshur, son of Shem (Gen. 10:22). Ibn
Ezra thought that the Ninevites had worshipped the
true God. But, however uncertain they may have been
as to the designs of God, the Jews understood Jonah. As
early as the second mid-century C.E., Rabbi Nathan
(Jonathan) stated that Jonah boarded the ship to drown
himself in the sea for the sake of Israel, not to flee from
the presence of God.

The Church fathers accepted the Jewish interpretation but turned it against its authors. Theodore of Mopsuestia says Jonah was sent to Nineveh because the Jews
refused to listen to the prophets, and the book about
Jonah was written to teach a lesson to the stiff-necked
people. Nineveh believed, says Jerome, but incredulous
Israel persists in refusing to acknowledge Jesus. Ephraem
describes how the saved Ninevites desired to learn righteousness from the holy people of their missionary. But
Jonah feared lest they should see the iniquity of Israel.
From the top of a mountain on the border of the Holy
Land, the Ninevites, who accompanied the prophet home,
saw with horror the abominations of Israel: graven images, the high places, the adoration of calves set up by
Jeroboam (I Kings 12:29), and the public and private
wickedness castigated by the prophets. "Perhaps this people is going to be extirpated in place of Nineveh which
has not been overthrown."

Thus taunted, the Jews tried to rebut the charge. They imagined that Jerusalem also, even before Nineveh, had once returned to God after admonition by Jonah. They also pretended that the repentance of Nineveh was not sincere. This polemic may go back to Rabbi Akiba himself. Yet in the fasting service for rain, the Ninevites were named as the paragons of efficacious repentance. Jesus was probably neither the sole nor the first preacher to warn his audience that at the last judgment the men of Nineveh would condemn unrepenting Israel (Matt. 12:41). An anonymous statement in the Midrash on Lamentations opposes Nineveh, which became contrite at the first call, and Jerusalem, which never heeded the prophets sent to her "in the morning and in the evening"; it asserts that therefore the Jews were exiled. In the twelfth century the learned Jewish commentator David Kimchi (c. 1160–1240) of Narbonne repeated this statement and suggested that the Book of Jonah had been written to show an example to Israel.

Rupert of Deutz (near Cologne), who died in 1145, was one of the finest Christian commentators on Scripture. Following and appreciating the Jewish view on Jonah, he states that the prophet refused to follow his call not through absence of faith, but out of piety to his people. And he finely observed that for this reason God had not been very angry at Jonah. The learned abbot echoes the criticism of Jonah already proffered in the times of Rabbi Akiba, that Jonah was jealous for the glory of the son (Israel) but not for the glory of the father (God).

As early as the end of the fourth century, however, some Christians contended that Jonah was not grieved for Israel's sake but begrudged the Gentiles their salvation. As Augustine explains, Jonah prefigures the carnal people of Israel who were sad at the redemption and deliverance of the nations. Jerome, as well as Cyril of Alexandria, his younger contemporary, rejected this malevolent interpretation, because in the Church view Jonah was a prefiguration of Christ. Jerome reminds his Christian readers that Jesus wept over Jerusalem (Luke 19:41) and that he said (Mark 7:27) that the children (Israel) should be fed first and their bread should not be cast to the dogs (the Gentiles). Jonah did not envy the deliverance of Nineveh, but wanted his own country not to perish.

Luther in his German explanation of Jonah (1526) revived and sharpened the opinion condemned by Jerome and virtually all medieval commentators. He asserted that the prophet was an enemy of Nineveh and held the Jewish "carnal" opinion that the Deity was the God of the Jews alone. Therefore, Jonah refused a share in the divine mercy to the Gentiles. Yet Luther was a man of free and zealous spirit, who intentionally mistranslated a line in Jonah's prayer because, as he says, he could see Jonah inside the whale and feel his despondency. Luther later spoke of "the surpassing majesty of the Prophet Jonah," and was ashamed of his commentary upon this prophet. Luther wondered how Jonah could presume to command God Almighty. "It is a great mystery."

Luther's Commentary on Jonah did not affect the exegetes of Scripture. They continued to reproduce one of two traditional views. Calvin insists that Jonah did not want to be known as a false prophet. Bossuet, in 1695, agrees with the father of French Protestantism. Thomas Hobbes (1651) speaks of Jonah's "forwardness and disputing God's commandment." A century later, the leading Lutheran exegete does not even mention Luther's opinion, but states that God in sending Jonah wanted to display His universal mercy and castigate Israel.

When J. G. Carpzow published his huge handbook (1757) the philosophical Age of Enlightenment had already blossomed. The philosophers, however, paid no attention to the problem of Jonah's flight, though from Bayle's Dictionary (1696) to Voltaire's *La Bible enfin expliquée* they made fun of Jonah's whale. Shaftesbury (1711) facetiously likened the unwilling prophet to a pettish truant boy, and Diderot (1746) opined that in his time Jonah would be sent to an institution. Thomas Paine in his *Age of Reason* (1793) thinks that the Book of Jonah was written to satirize the malignant character of a Bible prophet or a predicting priest. The fiery rationalist probably did not know that the latitudinarian J. G. Herder had already advanced a similar idea: the Book of Jonah was a fictitious tale describing the faults of the prophetic calling and a prophet afraid of losing his reputation.

Yet, however strange it may appear on first view, the ideology of Enlightenment led to the renewal of the almost forgotten hypothesis of Augustine and Luther: Jonah was an enemy of the Gentiles. How did it happen? To understand the universal acceptance of this view, we need to make an excursion into the field of intellectual history.

The Enlightenment

English freethinkers and French rationalists sought a natural system of morality fit for all men and times. They condemned positive religions whose sectarianism divided mankind and whose pretensions were not founded on argument. Without test of reason, as P. Anet said in 1744 (*The Resurrection Reconsidered*), Christian faith would be "equal to the religion of Juppiter Amon and the Ephesian Diana."

Testing the Scripture, they found it wanting: Scripture did not satisfy the demands of heart and reason. The Deists never tired of exposing the incredibility and absurdity of the biblical books. Their observations were often brilliant and sometimes anticipated later discoveries. For instance, their animus led them to assert the authenticity of the Phoenician cosmogony, quoted by a Greek author of the second century C.E., and its anteriority to Mosaic revelations. The texts of the second millennium B.C.E. found some thirty years ago at Rash Shamra (ancient Ugarit) in Syria substantiated Voltaire in this regard.

Yet the criticism of the Deists was haphazard, arbitrary, and superficial. Engaged in the holy war against superstition, they had no concern for exact interpretation of texts which appeared to them as tissues of unbelievable fables and vile errors. They were no scholars and addressed their works to gentlefolk, not to pedants and bluestockings. The Deists, always ready to attack the heavens, did not undermine the powers that be on the earth. They respected the fabric of eighteenth-century society. It was proper to meet an archbishop atheist, but a coiffeur who said that he too did not believe in God was a joke. The Deists recognized the utility of religious beliefs for public order. Jacques Necker, a banker and royal minister, stressed this point on the eve of the French Revolution (*De l'importance des opinions religieuses*, 1788) and so did the first President of the United States in his *Farewell Address* (1796). Both, directly or indirectly, were influenced by Polybius and Cicero. In

the vein of the latter, Conyers Middleton, Anglican cler-
gyman and theologian (1685–1750), could quietly say
that even if Christianity were an imposture, it was reason-
able to keep it as a state religion since no society can do
without religion.[2] Gibbon only half jokingly wrote to
Lord Sheffield in 1791 that he had criticized the primi-
tive Church because he was "attached to the old pagan
establishment."

Useful as it may be, the positive religion was not
true in the eyes of the rationalists and for them fulfilled
no need. They were ready to give God His passport
and conduct Him politely to the frontier of reason.
From his dungeon André Chénier reproached the Deity
for tolerating Robespierre's Reign of Terror (1794):

> *Tu ne crains pas qu'au pied de ton superbe trône,*
> *Spinosa, te parlant tout bas,*
> *Vienne te dire encore: "Entre nous je soupçonne,*
> *Seigneur, que vous n'existez pas."*

Chénier was guillotined two days before the fall of
Robespierre, who asserted that atheism was aristocratic
while the idea of the just God who protects and avenges
the oppressed favored the people.[3]

The Aufklärung

To become accepted in academic circles, biblical
criticism by freethinkers had to pass through the hands
of German professors. The essential difference between
the German *Aufklärung* and the Enlightenment was that

English and French freethinkers from Lord Herbert of Cherbury to Voltaire and Thomas Paine were unattached writers who addressed themselves to the aristocracy and the intellectuals who gravitated around the great houses. Oxford and Cambridge, not to speak of the Sorbonne, were dead set against biblical criticism. Richard Bentley, greatest classical scholar of his age (1662–1742), tore to pieces the *Discourse on Freethinkers* of Anthony Collins. The Deists praised Newton as the founder of mechanical cosmology. The founder himself believed that Moses had an inkling of Newtonian doctrine. As late as 1869 a German author could state that English theologians of his time were bound to the traditional view of the Bible almost more closely than the Roman Catholics.[4]

In Germany the universities propagated the message of the *Aufklärung*. It was Kant, Professor at Königsberg, who answered the question: *Was ist Aufklärung?* The most uncompromising German critic of Old and New Testament was H. S. Reimarus (1694–1768), Professor at Hamburg. German theologians, too, were carried away by the spirit of the *Aufklärung*. They, however, in contradistinction to English and French Deists wrote not for leisured gentlemen but for other professors and for former, present, and future students. The gibes, the aphorisms, and the shoddy learning of the Enlightenment were here out of place. The reader demanded earnest approach and exact scholarship. Thus, inspired by French and English free thought, men like J. D. Michaelis (1717–1791) and J. D. Eichhorn (1752–1827) established the foundations of modern biblical scholarship. But these learned men were also missionaries of the *Aufklärung*. Therefore, they almost unwittingly gave a bias to *Bibel-wissenschaft*.

The theologians of the *Aufklärung* took their official religion seriously. There was no flippancy. Radical

as they could be in the realm of pure thought, these professors were assiduous churchgoers, pious in their own
way, and docile to the authority, secular and ecclesiastic.
The *Aufklärung*, in contradistinction to the *siècle des
lumières*, did not want to "crush" the dogmatic religion
(Voltaire: *écrasez l'infâme*), but to reform the Evangelical Church. Accordingly, the *Aufklärung* differed from
the *siècle des lumières* in the appreciation of Jewish and
Christian revelations. The Deists rejected the idea of revelation addressed to a particular people. Jewish monotheism annoyed them. Following Celsus and Julian the
Apostate, the famous pagan opponents of Christianity,
the Deists described the God of the Bible as the tutelary
Deity of a little tribe. When a fashionable and, in his way,
a pious English writer of today speaks of the emergence
of a single and unique Deity in the "Syriac" civilization,
he probably unknowingly echoes the unbelievers who
taught Gibbon. Lord Bolingbroke (1678–1751) had already guessed that the "discovery" of monotheism "was
made in Egypt, and in all the eastern nations that were
famous for learning and knowledge."

Accordingly, the Deists, with a few exceptions such
as John Toland, violently attacked the Mosaic revelation
addressed to only one elect nation (here, again, they
followed Celsus and Julian), but believed or pretended
to believe that their universal religion had already been
intimated in the Gospels. "No system can be more simple
and plain than that of natural religion as it stands in the
Gospel." Yet they knew, as John Selden said, that Christianity was only a "reformed Judaism." And "the New
Testament supposes the truth of the Old," wrote Lord
Bolingbroke. Heaping up abuse against the Old Testament
in the line of Celsus, Porphyry, and Julian, they demol-
ished the outer line of Christian defense. De Mirbaud
(*Opinions des anciens sur les Juifs*, 1769) collects anti-

Jewish statements in Greek and Latin literatures. But his aim is to show that "the universal contempt for the Jews" is not the result "of the curse which Jesus Christ called down upon this race." In fact, the Deists are no less mordant when speaking of Jesus and the Apostles than they are in their treatment of Moses and the prophets. Bolingbroke writes of "the most artful behavior" of Jesus, objects to the doctrine of redemption, and, echoing pagan polemics, asks whether mankind was more in need of salvation four thousand years after their race began than at any other period. De Mirbaud (*Réflexions impartiales sur les Evangiles*, 1769) states that Jesus, though preaching love to one's enemy, never spoke lovingly of the Pharisees, his own enemies.

The *Aufklärung*, in agreement with the Enlightenment, asserted that a belief repugnant to the religion of nature ought to be rejected as untrue. The Deists regarded both the Synagogue and the Church as untrue. But the theologians of the *Aufklärung*, who had both practical and psychological motives for defending their own official creed, found the religion of reason expressed in the pristine, albeit now depraved, doctrine of the established religion.

Moses Mendelssohn identified the religion of reason with that of the Synagogue. Immanuel Kant proclaimed that moral religion begins with Christianity. Which of these philosophers was right? If the religious doctrine had to pass the test of reason, Lavater was justified in demanding that Mendelssohn refute the truth of Christianity or accept it. Mendelssohn prudently escaped the horns of the dilemma by defending the Old Testament. Protestant theologians could not get away from the problem so easily. Their faith being based on the testimony of Scripture which includes both the Old and the New Testaments, they had to explain before the tribunal of reason why they followed Jesus and forsook Moses. Thus, the German theologians had to disparage the Old Testament as incompatible with the religion of reason, to make it appear that the new dispensation alone agreed with rational religion. For some 150 years the "enlightened" and "liberal" Protestantism of German universities, from Semler (1725–1791) and Eichhorn to Wellhausen and Harnack, was inherently and almost necessarily opposed to the Old Testament in order to salvage the residue of evangelical faith. With the *Aufklärung*, the spirit of Marcion, the fiery heretic who (c. 150) rejected the God of the Old Testament, conquered German Protestant theology.

Basing themselves on the deistic creed that the universal values of morality were inscribed by the Supreme Being on the minds of all men, and the deistic principle of ethical criticism of Scripture, and believing that the mark of true revelation was its utility in promoting the natural system of morality (this pragmatic view was a feature of German pietism), the theologians of the *Aufklärung* declared that the Old Testament was purely Jewish, but the message of the Gospel universal.

In this view, the meaning of the Book of Jonah appeared clear and simple. The prophets were wise men who defended the doctrine of nature against priestly superstition. Jonah was a narrow-minded sectarian but the author of his story spoke for universal morality. To the most prominent exegetes of the *Aufklärung*, such as J. S. Semler (1773), J. D. Michaelis (1782), and J. D. Eichhorn (1783), Jonah exemplified the Jewish fanaticism which begrudged God's mercy to the Gentiles. The Book of Jonah was written as an admonition to intolerant Israel.

To gain its almost universal acceptance among exegetes, however, this interpretation required a second modification. The writings of H. E. G. Paulus may illustrate the change. Born in the age of tolerance (1761), Paulus died in the age of German nationalism (1851). He was known for his naive defense of the miraculous stories in the Gospels: Jesus did not walk on the sea (Matt. 14:25) but along the shore of the sea. In 1794, Paulus wrote that the Book of Jonah was written to explain why prophecies may remain unfulfilled. His view was restated several times by later German scholars, but with a significant twist: the Book of Jonah explains to the Jews why the prophecies of doom against the Gentiles have not been realized as yet.

Paulus himself, in 1831, published a pamphlet against Jewish emancipation under the significant title: *Die jüdische Nationalabsonderung*. He did not oppose the Jewish religion as such, but the observance of Mosaic law: such institutions as circumcision or the observance of the Sabbath make the Jews a separate people. He does not, however, demand from the Catholics that they abandon the adoration of the Host and their allegiance to the Pope. As Gabriel Riesser, a leader in the fight for emancipation, had already noted in answering Paulus, the Jews were no longer disliked because of "religious hate," but their peculiarity became an affront to German nationalism. Baptism was now not a proof of true faith but of national solidarity. In this view, Jonah appears as the typical asocial Jew who is hostile to all other nations. The atheist Bruno Bauer (1838), the "liberal" Protestant Friedrich Bleek (1860), and the pious C. F. Keil (1866) agree on this point. Under the influence of German universities, this conception, though expressed less crudely, now dominated the interpretation of the Book of Jonah. According to an authoritative American work which in 1957 summarized how contemporary scholarship interpreted the Bible, for Jonah the mercy of God was a fine thing when it was directed to Israel, but a distasteful thing when directed toward Israel's enemies. The intention of the author of Jonah, we are told, was to protest against the nationalist exclusivism of the Jewish outlook.

The Fold of the True Faith

Biased exegetes, however learned, are likely to misunderstand the book they seek to explain. For Jews, as for Christians and Muslims, the unity of mankind is realizable only within the fold of the true faith. This principle is a corollary of monotheism. Bishop John Hooper explained in a sermon that God had sent Jonah to Nineveh to declare that the works of the Law were not necessary for salvation. Hooper ended his life on the stake in 1555, under the reign of Mary Tudor, for refusing to be reconciled to the Papist Church. For him no redemption was possible outside his own truth. In fact, the expression of universal neighborly love of the Christian Church is the prayer of intercession, already attested in the New Testament (I Tim. 2:4), that all men will be saved by the knowledge of the truth. In the same way the Jews believed, as Rabbi Eliezer of Modiin (c. 100 C.E.) put it, that at the end of time Israel will be saved with her God and the heathens condemned with their idols. But Israel was a standing witness of the truth to the pagan world, and the Gentiles were not precluded from joining the true faith. The sailors of Jonah's ship, although heathen, offered a sacrifice to the Lord and made vows. When, after the destruction of the Temple in 70 C.E. the Jews themselves could no longer sacrifice to God, the rabbis continued to encourage God-fearing Gentiles to sacrifice to the Lord outside the Holy Land. A rabbinical text, coming perhaps from a missionary sermon, states that four classes of persons belong to God: the Israelites who have not sinned, the Israelites who have repented, the proselytes, and the Gentiles who fear Heaven.

The Ninevites who believed the word of Jonah and acknowledged the power of Jonah's God were among those Gentiles who feared the Lord. Ibn Ezra aptly quotes the case of Jethro (Exod. 18:11) who inferred from the miracle of the Exodus that the God of Moses is greater than all (other) gods. Modern scholars maliciously or naively imagine that the author of Jonah portrayed the heathen as accessible to the divine truth in contrast to the vindictive narrow-mindedness of the Jewish prophet. In fact, the author shows that even the heathen, who by revering the lying vanities of idols forsake their own mercy (2:9), are sometimes compelled to revere the omnipotent God of Jonah and to acclaim His miracles. As stated above, the morality play of Jonah has a cast of three characters: God, the prophet, and the Ninevites. David Kimchi observed to his great surprise that there is nothing about Israel. The opposition between Israel and the Gentiles is introduced by commentators who find more than is really there.

Conditional and Unconditional Fates

Six or seven centuries separated the author of Jonah from his earliest rabbinical exegetes. He wrote after 612 when Nineveh, the Assyrian capital since Sennacherib (705–681), was destroyed: "Nineveh was a great city before the Lord" (Jonah 3:3). The book was written under Persian rule: the edict of penance for the Ninevites was issued "by the king and his grandees" (Jonah 3:7). The cooperation of high lords in royal legislation, unknown to both Jews and Assyrians, was a Persian procedure (cf. Ezra 7:14; Daniel 6:17; Esther 1:13). Jonah says (1:9) that he worships YHWH, the God of Heaven —an epithet of the Deity that was popular in the fifth century B.C.E. The other terminus is the Book of Tobit, which quotes Jonah, and was written in the fourth century. Thus the Book of Jonah was written in the fifth century.

This means that the author of Jonah was unlike the rabbis; for them prophesying was a thing of the past, having ceased, they believed, with Haggai, Zechariah, and Malachi, that is, about 500 B.C.E. The author of Jonah still saw the oraclemongers in hairy mantles, their faces marked by wounds self-inflicted in trance. He still listened to their frenzied messages (Zech. 13:4). And he represented Jonah as a prophet, that is, as a man who foretells events.

Strange as it may appear to us, all peoples of antiquity firmly believed that signs (for instance, the aspect of liver in a sacrificed animal) or inspired men could foretell the future. The soothsayer was consulted on every important occasion. The usual objection to prophecy advanced by skeptic philosophers of Greece was that the believer in divination pretends to modify the foreordained causality which he postulates by his inquiry. But this argument is fallacious. The man who listens to a weather forecast hopes not to change the weather but to adjust his plans to it. Foretelling likewise can help avoid pitfalls on the road into the future. Fatality is conditional. The predicted event will happen, if. . . . Laius was advised by Apollo not to have children. Trying to circumvent the Fates, Laius exposed the new-born Oedipus. As the Stoic philosopher Chrysippus (280–207) explains, if Apollo had not given the oracle, Oedipus would have known his parents and avoided killing his father and marrying his mother. Apollo knew that Laius would disobey and gave the oracle to start the chain of events so that the fate would be fulfilled. Yet Laius could have escaped his fate by not begetting a child. Accordingly, inquiries addressed to a soothsayer or to the prophet of the Lord presupposed the bifurcation of the road into the future (*duplex eventus*): "Shall I go to battle against Ramoth-Gilead or shall I forbear?" (I Kings 22:6). Further, the recipient of a prediction was free not to follow the oracular advice. A governor in the kingdom of Mari in the eighteenth century B.C.E. communicated a prophecy to his master and added: "May my lord do whatever he thinks right." Before the battle of Thermopylae in 480 B.C.E. the seer Megistias read in the entrails of sacrificial victims that the defenders of the pass would all fall. He sent away his son but stayed himself. As his funerary inscription says, "though he knew unerringly that the hostile fates were nearing, he did not dare abandon the captains of Sparta." [5]

This kind of prediction which, like our weather forecasts, gives man an alternative, was called by the Greeks "conditional fate" (fata conditionalia). To it, Greek theory opposed "declaratory destiny" (fata denunciativa) which works like a spell. Willy-nilly, Macbeth will be Thane of Cawdor and King of Scotland. The Pythia declared that Gyges, who had murdered his king, would reign in Lydia, but that divine punishment would fall on Gyges' fifth descendant. This descendant was Croesus, doomed thus long before his birth. The raving mouth of the Sibyl uttered words which foreordained events a thousand years ahead, according to Heraclitus, a contemporary of the author of Jonah. "The reporting servant of Phoebus" announced doom, like the great prophets of Israel. "She vaticinated the overthrow of Greek cities, foreign invasions, and fall of empires."

The Hebrew prophets were not only soothsayers to whom men went to inquire of God (I Sam. 9:9) but, above all, messengers of His will. Admonishing Israel, they conjured fata conditionalia. Thus says the Lord to the house of Israel: seek Me and live, and do not . . . enter into Gilgal . . . for Gilgal shall surely go into exile . . ." (Amos 5:4). "If you are willing and obedient, you shall eat the good of the land, but if you refuse and rebel, you shall be devoured by the sword. For the mouth of the Lord has spoken" (Isa. 1:19).

At other times, like the Sibyl, they declared the immutable and unavoidable fata denunciativa.

From his village south of Bethlehem, Amos darted dire words at Damascus and other heathen cities. "Thus says the Lord . . . I will send fire into the house of

Hazael, and it shall devour the palaces of Ben Hadad" (1:4). In the same vein, Nahum in the name of the Lord announced to Nineveh: "I will make thy grave." Such words are not guesses like a weather forecast, but stimuli which evoke the dormant fates. King Ahab of Israel hated Micaiah who prophesied not good but evil (I Kings 22). In Jerusalem, Isaiah was asked to foretell "agreeable things" (Isa. 30:10). In Homer, King Agamemnon reproaches the seer Calchas that he did not once speak a favorable oracle nor did he bring one to pass.

The rabbis and the Christian writers, commenting on Jonah in the light of their own experiences and according to their own needs, saw Jonah as a missionary who, as Jerome says, demanded repentance worthy of his preaching. In other words, according to this interpretation Jonah's prediction to Nineveh was conditional: repent or else. This is already the image of Jonah in the Gospels and in the Greek version of his book, where Jonah is bidden to "proclaim in the city." But the Hebrew text states that the prophet was commanded to "cry against" Nineveh, and he "cried against" her: "Yet forty days, and Nineveh shall be overthrown." As Augustine says: "Jonah announced not mercy but the coming anger" (*annuntiavit Jonas non misericordiam sed iram futuram*). In a terse Latin sentence, the great exegete formulates the dialectical problem of Jonah and of Jonah's tale. Jonah was not a missionary preacher threatening divine punishment as *fata conditionalia*. Herald of God's wrath, Jonah declared the immutable and inevitable *fata denunciativa:* "Yet forty days, and Nineveh shall be overthrown." Nineveh was like Sodom: the sinfulness of Nineveh is described, as David Kimchi noted, in the same words as are used in Genesis about Sodom. Long before Kimchi, Cyril of Alexandria asked why Jonah had been sent to faraway Nineveh and not to Tyre or some other

heathen city. The church father explains: Nineveh was
a new Sodom. Yet, the Lord did not rain brimstone and
fire out of heaven upon Nineveh. Why?

False Prophets and
False Oracles

The true seer speaks truth. An Assyrian diviner
writes: "The message that I had sent you is the truth."
God let none of Samuel's words fall to the ground, and
brought all that he said surely to pass. If a prophet speaks
in the name of God and the prediction is not fulfilled,
"that is the thing which the Lord has not spoken."

Jonah went to Nineveh, announcing in the name of
God that in forty days the city would be overthrown.
Yet, the *fata denunciativa* did not materialize. Was he a
false prophet, who only pretended to speak in the name of
God? No, the miracle of the great fish vouches for his
authority. As he explains to God and to the reader, he
suspected from the beginning that his oracle would not
be realized. But a seer whose prediction was not realized
appeared as a false prophet. Socrates declared that the
Deity gave him signs. Socrates would have appeared as a
fool and braggart, says Xenophon, if he foretold things
as revealed to him by the Deity and then was refuted by
events. That happened to Jeremiah, who became a laugh-
ingstock when his predictions were not immediately realized, and he cursed the day he was born (Jer. 20:14).
The Deist Toland commented that this passage proves

the prophets were dupes or duped. Accordingly, the earliest extant exegesis of the Book of Jonah presents him as fleeing from his call because, being a prophet, he knew beforehand that his threats against Nineveh would remain vain and that he would be derided as a false prophet. Preserved in the homily on Jonah by Philo, this interpretation was accepted by some Church fathers and, it would seem, by some rabbis. It reappears in medieval Jewish compilations, was disputed by Ibn Ezra, and was received favorably by the great theologian Saadia (822–942) and by Rashi (1040–1105), the foremost Jewish commentator on Scripture.

Viewed in this light, Jonah had been placed in a great quandary. Jerome formulates the prophet's problem: he could say that God is merciful, but then the Ninevites would not have repented; or he could say that God is implacable. He said the latter, and thus predicted falsely, and was indignant that God made him a liar. In Philo, God answers Jonah: "Thou mayest say, O prophet, . . . from My humiliation didst thou receive honor." "If thou art perturbed about the falseness of thy proclamation, thy accusation is against Me and not thee, O prophet. For thou preached not what thou wished but what thou received." [6]

Thus it was not the prophet but the divine word which was false. Yet, from earliest times men have assumed that in this sublunar world, full of errors and falsehoods, the divine pronouncement alone is true and steadfast. As far back as the third millennium B.C.E., a Sumerian hymn proclaims that the word of the supreme god Enlil is holy and unchangeable. In the days of the Second Isaiah, the mother of the last Babylonian king, Nabonidus (556–539), in a remarkable document of deep and personal piety, referred to Enlil "whose word is not spoken twice." Kings imitated gods. Esarhaddon, King

of Assyria (681–669), proclaimed that his word was unalterable. The plot of the Book of Esther hinges on the
principle that the royal word cannot be countermanded.

The Greeks did not believe kings, and some Greeks
dared to doubt the veracity of gods. As early as 546, long
before the Book of Jonah was written, the reputation
of Apollo of Delphi received a blow. The Delphic oracle
encouraged Croesus of Lydia, a benefactor of Delphi, in
ambiguous words ("if you cross the river Halys, you
shall overthrow a mighty power") to make war on the
Persian King Cyrus. Croesus lost the war and the kingdom, and the Greek god seemed to have betrayed the
piety of his generous worshipper. In the pages of Herodotus, written a century later, we can still perceive the
impression that the failure of Apollo made on the contemporaries of Croesus, and we learn of subterfuges used
to explain away this failure.

Several decades later, in a tragedy of Aeschylus,
Thetis, the mother of Achilles, complained of Apollo's
duplicity. He had promised Achilles a long life, and then
slew him. And she had believed that Phoebus' mouth was
without falsehood, and that he neither changed in himself nor deluded others by visions and signs.

But Thetis was mistaken. Aeschylus himself witnessed
how Apollo changed his word. Before the Persian War,
the god told the Athenian envoys that their city was
doomed. When they insisted on receiving a more favorable oracle, the god relented and gave his "adamant word"
that a "wooden wall" would not be destroyed. That
was understood to refer to the wooden ships of the
Athenian navy—and at Salamis in 480 B.C.E. the Athenians destroyed the Persian fleet.

Some devout souls in Greece had recourse to the
theory of the useful lie. "The mouth of the god who does
not lie does not abstain from righteous deceit." But Plato

insisted that the gods are by nature incapable of lying, and that the tales of misleading oracles had been invented by poets.

But Jerusalem was no Athens. No poets there blamed Heaven's will. Everybody knew that the word of God which is gone forth does not come back (Isa. 45:23), and that the Lord changes not (Mal. 3:6). "God is not a man that He should lie, nor the son of man that he should repent" (Num. 23:19). Some six centuries after the author of the Book of Jonah, the author of the Epistle to the Hebrews (6:18) asserted that God is sure in His promises to Abraham since it is "impossible for God to lie." Alluding to this passage in a firework of brilliant rhetoric, Augustine proves to the pagans, who deny the possibility of bodily resurrection, that only one thing is impossible to God: to lie. And God has promised the coming to life of the dead.[7]

Accordingly, to annul the result of His decree, God had to change its direction. Nathan predicted a dire punishment on the House of David. The king repented and the prophet uttered a new oracle: David shall live, but the child he begot in sin "shall surely die" (II Sam. 12). Isaiah told the sick King Hezekiah that he would die. Hezekiah prayed and the word of the Lord came to the prophet announcing that fifteen years were added to the life of the pious king (Isa. 38). When Hezekiah sinned again, Isaiah announced that the Jews would be carried to Babylon. The king meekly accepted the oracle if there should be peace in his days. In the same way, God does not revoke but postpones the announced punishment of Ahab: "In his son's days I will bring evil upon his house" (I Kings 21:20). According to the rabbis, if Israel repents, God's harsh decree is not canceled but is directed against the heathen. In his sermon on the capture of Rome by Alaric in 410 C.E., Augustine reports

that a soldier received revelation, probably in 398, of
the coming destruction of Constantinople by fire from
heaven. Like Nineveh, he says, the city turned to penitence and was saved. But to accredit the oracle, on the
predicted day a fiery cloud hung over the city.

Thus, the pious readers of old who, unlike modern
commentators, took God's word and words seriously,
could not believe that the oracle of Jonah against Nineveh
remained unfulfilled. "All the things which the prophets
of Israel spoke, whom God sent, shall befall," says the
author of Tobit, "and nothing shall be diminished of all
words, and all things shall come to pass in their season."
Thus Tobit, who died some years before the fall of Nineveh (612 B.C.E.), advises his children to flee Assyria: "I believe the word of God upon Nineveh which Jonah spoke."
The Book of Tobit was written in the fourth century
B.C.E., that is, at a time when even the location of the
former Assyrian capital was forgotten. When Josephus
wrote at the end of the first century C.E., there was a
new (Greek) city of Nineveh. So Josephus says that
Jonah predicted that Assyria would be deprived of the
domination of Asia. Some rabbis thought that Nineveh
only received a reprieve, and the word of Jonah was
brought to pass forty years (forty days in Jonah's oracle)
later. Jerome knows this view; he states that the Ninevites,
having returned to their sinful ways, were then condemned definitively.

The Unfulfilled Prophecy

The pious authors of these ingenious hypotheses tried to read between the lines. Yet they point to the puzzle which must perplex any attentive reader of Jonah. Commentators of old, such as Kimchi, wondered at the abruptness of the tale, and supposed it came from a lost book on Jonah. Yet the biblical story is not about a prophet but about an unfilfilled prophecy. God's wonderful graciousness here explains the failure of Jonah's prediction. The scheme though not the intent of the tale is that of a tract which vindicates the trustworthiness of divine oracles.

How can God's word remain unfulfilled? When Jeremiah's dire oracles against Jerusalem seemed to be in vain, the prophet expostulated with God: "O Lord, Thou hast enticed me . . ." (Jer. 20:7). Yet it was the same Jeremiah who, challenging the determinism of the *fata denunciativa*, offered a new perspective in theology. Observing how the potters refashioned the marred clay, he discovered that God can act in the same way. The divine decision is not unalterable, and the fate is changeable. God may speak against a nation but if it turns from evil God will repent of the harm that He thought to do unto it. Likewise, if a nation does evil, He will repent of the favor He said He would bestow (Jer. 18). Repeated by later prophets such as Ezekiel (38), this theory of the conditional prophecy became a part of Jewish and then Christian theology. The oracle is not automatically effective. Its realization depends on man's conduct. God pardoned Nineveh not because of a faulty judgment in giving the oracle of destruction, says Jerome, but because the Ninevites had changed their ways.

Jeremiah hoped against hope that in the last hour his people might be converted and the final doom turned aside. He published a collection of his prophecies so that the house of Judah, hearing all the evils which God devised against it, might return from the "evil ways" (Jer. 36:3), and, accordingly, he understood the words of the prophets before him as conditional foretelling (Jer. 25:4).

This anthropocentric theory, which made fate a function of man's varying behavior, agreed with man's hopes. In 609 Jeremiah was threatened with the death penalty since he "prophesied against the city." His accusers believed in the efficacy of oracles. But some of the elders quieted the hostile crowd, quoting the similar oracle of Micah (3:12), which did not materialize since King Hezekiah supplicated the Lord (Jer. 26).

Few among us care to remember, however, the other part of Jeremiah's startling theory: that God's promises no less than His threats are conditioned on man's conduct. We like to believe, with Rabbi Johanan quoting Rabbi Jose, that every favorable word issued from the mouth of God, even if it was given conditionally, was never withdrawn.

Jonah vs. Jeremiah: Herald vs. Watchman

The fate of the Ninevites exemplified for the rabbis the conditional nature of decrees of doom. In his commentary on Jonah, Tanchum ben Joseph of Jerusalem restates this principle. But if it is so, he asks in perplexity, why did Jonah flee, and why was he angered by the remission of punishment after the amendment of the Ninevites? The answer (which a Jew of the thirteenth century could not conceive) is that Jonah refused to accept the perspective of Jeremiah and Ezekiel, in which the prophet is no longer God's herald, but a watchman who blows a horn to warn his people of coming danger (Ezek. 3:16; 33:1–9). This image means, as Jerome explains Ezekiel, that the prophets foretell punishment to make it unnecessary. But, as Cyril of Alexandria, following a hint by Philo, makes Jonah remonstrate with God: "Why hast thou ordered me to proclaim the catastrophe in vain?" In the same manner, the rabbis refer to two contradictory oracles about Hezekiah (Isa. 38) and make Isaiah protest to God: "First Thou sayest one thing to me, and now another."

Jonah, who rightly foretold the recovery of the borders of Israel (II Kings 14:25), was unwilling to proclaim an oracle which he knew beforehand would not be realized. "For I know that thou art a gracious God and compassionate, long-suffering, and abundant in mercy, and relentest thee in mercy and relentest thee from evil." Except for the last one, these attributes of God come from a longer list in Exodus 34, a familiar passage often referred to in other passages of the Bible. A Psalmist in distress would repeat only the appellations describing God's mercifulness (Ps. 103:8), while Nahum (1:3) in condemning Nineveh emphasizes that God though long-suffering will not clear the guilty. Jonah quotes the formula in the exact wording given it by Joel (2:13).

Such literary allusions served to make clear the thought of the writer. An invasion of locusts was for Joel a signal of the coming day of the Lord's judgment. He called on Jerusalem to repent and trust in the Lord, "for He is gracious . . . and abundant in mercy, and relenting from evil." These last words are Joel's addition to the common list of divine attributes. "Who knows, He may turn and change His mind." The author of Jonah's tale makes the king of the Ninevites repeat this expression of hope: "Who knows, He may turn and change His mind, the God." But the prophet Jonah quotes from Joel's description of God not to encourage the penitents but to explain his flight from the mission which will bring about repentance and thus cause God to relent from the evil He devised to do unto the sinners. It is this almost mechanical reciprocity between man's repent-ance and God's changing His mind that rouses the anger of the prophet Jonah.

The divine mercy was no privilege of Israel. Gods of the nations, too, were compassionate and relenting from evil. Had the author of Jonah visited Delos, he would have seen the idol of Apollo holding the Graces on his right hand and a bow and arrow in his left. The traditional explanation was that the Greek god was prompt to bestow grace and slow to chastise. On the banks of the Euphrates, in the valley of the Nile, and in the mountains of Asia Minor, repentant sinners humbled themselves and fervently trusted in the mercy of Ishtar or Ammon or Sabazios. The pagan gods often delayed the punishment of the wicked in order to allow them time to change their way of life. The evil deeds of the rebellious Babylonians provoked Marduk, the patron god of the city, to "frame evil" against her. In 689 Babylon was destroyed by the Assyrian king Sennacherib. But the heart of the merciful Marduk calmed, he felt compassion for his city—and Babylon was restored by Esarhaddon, in 680 B.C.E.

Like Babylon, Jerusalem learned both the righteous wrath and the wondrous grace of Heaven. After the return from the Exile, Zechariah (1:6) could remind his hearers that the words of the prophets had been fulfilled and that the Lord of Hosts had acted as He had proposed. For this reason, the author of Jonah could not send his hero to speak against Samaria or Jerusalem. Israel did not repent in time and had to experience divine wrath.

The question is, however, whether all sins are canceled through repentance. Referring to the example of Nineveh, the rabbis argued that God, having decreed the death of a man, will change His mind should the man repent. Yet they also knew of men who hoped that they might sin, repent, and be saved. Julian the Apostate was shocked at the Christian view that baptism cleansed of all sins. In his "Caesars" Julian describes a banquet of gods and deified emperors. Constantine, the first Christian emperor, is not among the gods, but wantonness leads him to profligacy, where he finds Jesus. Jesus calls every seducer, murderer, and criminal to approach without fear. "For with water I shall make him clean." Should one be guilty again, let him smite his breast and beat his head and he will be made clean again. Origen taught that repentance brings full pardon. For the function of sin is to teach humility. Punishment is educational. God is not really angry at the sinner. Like a father punishing his children, God desires only the salvation of men. The Devil himself will be converted in the end. In his commentary on Jonah, Jerome attacks this teaching of Origen which, if accepted, would destroy the fear of God. Hoping for divine mercy, men would be ready "to prepare their salvation with the Devil." And Jerome asks indignantly whether, in the end, there would be no difference between the Virgin Mary and a streetwalker, between Gabriel and the Devil, between martyrs and their torturers? God is both merciful and just.

Without trying to read between the lines, we may understand the prophet Jonah's protest against an idea that was popular in post-exilic Jerusalem that penitence reinstates the sinner in divine favor. "Return unto Me, and I shall return unto you" (Mal. 3:7).

Jonah and Jeremiah Reconciled

The author of Jonah's story makes a confrontation between the thesis of Jeremiah, Ezekiel, Joel, and Malachi that if you repent God will also change His mind, and the antithesis, of Jonah, that God's word once spoken must be steadfast. In the tale, God does not condescend to refute the outburst of His prophet. As Philo says, after having healed the Ninevites, God takes care of the affliction of Jonah by proposing the "parable," as Ibn

Ezra says, of the gourd. The withering of the plant which had sheltered him made Jonah angry. And God says to His prophet: You wanted to see spared the plant which you did not grow. Should I not spare a great city which I did create? The story ends on this rebuke.

The word "spare" (or "pity": *hus*) is a new one in the story. It does not bring about the mental association with forgiveness or repentance. It indicates a sovereign and arbitarary action: the enemy may or may not "spare" the population of a captured city (Jer. 21:7). The ideal king will "pity" the poor and needy (Ps. 72:13). The righteous Nehemiah ends his memoirs with the prayer that God may "have consideration" for him according to His great grace (*hesed*).

In using the term, the author of Jonah again models his narrative after Joel, who admonishes (2:17) Jerusalem to supplicate in the Temple: "Spare Thy people, O Lord." In this passage appeal is made not to God's forgiveness but to His concern for His own name in the sight of the nations. Thus Joel again helps the reader to understand the Book of Jonah.

The thesis of Jeremiah and the antithesis of the prophet Jonah are reconciled and surmounted in a so-to-say Hegelian synthesis by the author of the book, who, as the ancient Jewish commentators noted, wrote a parable for Jerusalem. Cyril of Alexandria wondered why Jonah had been sent to faraway Nineveh. It was, he says, to show that God's mercy saves even the worst sinners. The evil doings of Nineveh were remembered for centuries. An Egyptian story, written in the popular ("demotic") language and still copied under the Roman Emperor Augustus, contained a prophecy of an Assyrian invasion and of Egyptian gods being brought to Nineveh. Jeremiah (13:14) and Ezekiel (24:14) had predicted that God would not "spare" Jerusalem, and their oracles came to pass. To the restored and still sinful city, the author tells his parable. If God once did spare Nineveh, would He not save Jerusalem by His sovereign decision?

Omnipotent and Merciful

The Jews were not alone in being a chosen people. In fact, there has hardly ever been a tribe that was not elected by heaven. Israel was the Lord's people as Ashur was the city of the god Ashur. The Athenian lawgiver Solon, a contemporary of Jeremiah, spoke of his city in words that remind us of the admonitions of the Hebrew prophets. Our city, he says, will never be overthrown by the will of Zeus, "since Pallas Athene, whose hands are stretched out above [us]," protects it. The citizens themselves, by their cupidity and lawlessness, threaten the existence of Athens. The Jews were equally sure that the Lord protected Jerusalem: "Is not the Lord in the midst of us? No evil shall come upon us" (Mic. 3:11).

But while Pallas was unthinkable without the Athenians, and no people, as Jeremiah said, ever forsook their gods, Israel apostasized again and again, and the Lord was free to abandon His elected nation. The relation between the heavenly patron and a people was natural elsewhere, the connection between the Lord and Israel was of free choice. The Torah does not say why God called Abraham and not his brother Nahor, nor why, before the birth of the twins, He chose Jacob and not Esau. The Lord has chosen Israel by unmerited favor and, so to say, irrationally, because He loved her (Deut. 7:8), and the prophets know that some day He may not love her any longer (Hos. 9:15). God may cast off Jerusalem, the city He has chosen (II Kings 23:27) and reject Judah (Jer. 14:19).

The Jews were Abraham's sons but, as John the Baptist told them (Matt. 3:9), God was able to raise up children to Abraham out of stones. The Lord who led the Hebrews from Egypt also brought the Philistines from Caphtor and Aram from Kir (Amos 9:7). The claim of the Christian Church to be "the true Israel," which in God's favor has supplanted the deicide Israel, may be wrong, but it is not absurd, as would be the claims of some people that they and not the Assyrians were the people of the god Ashur. It is not an accident that the new faith was born in Palestine. There was no place for a new religion outside Israel.

The pagan gods were inseparable from their respective peoples since these gods were parts of nature, like the landscape of their cities. In all ancient mythologies, from India to Egypt and Greece, matter precedes the gods who are only the organizers of the universe. The cosmic order and its truths are above the gods as well as men. But the God of Abraham, of Isaac, and of Jacob is the Creator. When, in the Greek age, the Jews began to philosophize, they recognized this essential difference between the Lord and the pagan pantheon. The heroic Mother of Seven Sons slain by Antiochus IV, exhorting them to remain steadfast in the ancestral faith, speaks of God who created everything from nothing and concludes that He can also refashion the body after death. Paul repeats this reasoning: "God, who quickens the dead, and calls into existence things which do not exist." Christian apologists Justin, Theophilus, Athenagoras again and again stressed that the pagan gods did not exist at the beginning. As Hegel (1770–1831), who knew his Bible, noted: Nature, which in the East is the primary and fundamental existence, is depressed in the Bible to the condition of a mere creature. God is the absolute causality.

Apollo, unable to annul "the fated doom" of Croesus (the sin of his ancestor Gyges had fallen upon him), delayed the king's fall for three years and saved his life. Marduk could not blot out the sentence of seventy years of desolation which he wrote himself. But he turned upside down the clay tablet on which the sentence had been written, so that in the cuneiform characters the figure "70" now appeared as "11." But the God of Jonah could annul the judgment spoken by him on Nineveh at a whim.

Being the absolute causality (to speak with Hegel), the Lord is the only being that is really omnipotent. He does not even need to keep His word. In Philo's homily, the Lord admonishes Jonah: "I am the absolute autocrat, I who threatened the Ninevites. I had the authority to establish and to annul the law, and to change the death sentence." The rabbis in the same vein contrasted the human judge, who cannot revoke his sentence, and God, who can. "There is no answer to him who spoke—and there was the world. Thus, His every word is true, and every decision is just." As Calvin says: "Let us learn by the example of Jonah not to measure God's judgment by our own wisdom." This wise ignorance does not weigh down the author and the reader of Jonah. Heraclitus, a contemporary of the book, believed that Time (which changes everything) rules us in the same manner as a child plays draughts. Plato, paraphrasing Heraclitus, believed that we are marionettes in the hands of the gods, contrived as their toys or for some purpose of which we know nothing. But Jonah and his readers knew that their God, slow in anger and abounding in mercy, is no puppeteer, even if His ways are often incomprehensible to mortal mind. The story of Jonah teaches us that God is merciful, but He is merciful because He is Creator. As Kimchi, quoting Isaiah (43:7), puts it, God created men for His glory and He forgives them for the sake of His glory. In Augustinian terms: *gratia gratis datur*. A humanistic interpretation of the story of Jonah, judging it according to man's needs and mind, is fallacious. "Not to us, O Lord, not to us, but to thy Name give glory . . ." (Ps. 115).

The curious reader will find the annotation to this essay in its French version published in *Revue de l'histoire et de philosophie religieuses* (1965), pp. 232 ff. The notes that follow cover additional material in the English text.

1. This ingenious guess was first made, it seems, by Hermann von Hardt, *Aenigmata Jonae* (1719). See F. Vigouroux, *Les livres saints et la critique rationaliste* (1886), p. 317. J. Bodin (1530–96), in the beginning of his *Heptaplomeres*, parodies the tale of Jonah: an Egyptian mummy hidden in the lading of the ship provokes the fatal tempest.

2. C. Middleton, *Miscellaneous Works* III (1755), p. 56.

3. B. Récatas, *Mélanges Isidore Lévy* (1955), p. 517.

4. L. Diestel, *Geschichte des Alten Testaments in der christlichen Kirche* (1869), p. 619.

5. M. Noth, *Bulletin of the John Rylands Library*, xxxii (1950), p. 157. Herodotus 7.219, 228.

6. Philo's work on Jonah has been preserved in Armenian translation. As my colleague Nina Garsoian informs me, the Armenian word *kʿarozoutʿiur* means *praedicatio, praeconium*. H. Huebschmann, *Altarmenische Grammatik* (1897), p. 319, refers to the Aramaic word *karoza*. Cf. Dan. 3:4: "The herald (*karuza*) cried with force." Thus, in the Armenian Bible, the words *kʿaroz, kʿaroz-em* render the Greek terms *kerux, kerussein*, "herald." On the commentary of Tanchum ben Joseph of Jerusalem, cf. S. Poznanski, *Revue des études juives*, XL (1900), pp. 129 ff.; XLI (1900), pp. 45 ff.

7. Augustinus *De Civitate Dei*.

DANIEL
or
THE
FULFILLED
PROPHECY

Daniel and His Book

THE hero of the Book of Daniel is one of the Jews exiled in Babylonia, a soothsayer at the Babylonian court under Nebuchadnezzar (who died in 562 B.C.E.) and Belshazzar (who died in 539 B.C.E.), and at the Median and Persian courts in Babylon under "Darius the Mede" and Cyrus (who died in 529 B.C.E.).

Persons named Daniel ("God has judged") are mentioned in Babylonian records and in the Bible elsewhere. For instance, a signer of Nehemiah's covenant in 444 B.C.E. was a priest by the name of Daniel (Neh. 10:6). A Jewish oracle-monger of the same name may or may not have lived in Babylon at the time of King Nebuchadnezzar. Yet it is probable that the name of the hero of the Book of Daniel was chosen to bring to mind the Daniel spoken of in the Book of Ezekiel. The Lord says through the mouth of Ezekiel (14:4) that, "when a land sins against Me," these three alone, Noah, Job, and Daniel, by their righteousness would be able to escape the divine anger. At the court in Babylon, the seer Daniel again and again is in peril of life but because of his piety he is saved miraculously just as righteousness would have delivered his namesake. The seer Daniel is a "revealer of mysteries" (2:47) of the future to the kings. Ezekiel (28:3) scoffs at the ruler of Tyre who considers himself as wise as a god (and thus cognizant of the future). "Behold thou art wiser than Daniel. No secret is kept dark from thee." Ezekiel probably speaks of a legendary king of old, who rendered justice to the widow and the fatherless, and was celebrated in Canaanite epics. Yet the author and the readers of the Book of Daniel could not help but associate their Daniel with his namesake in the Book of Ezekiel.[1]

The Book of Daniel consists of two parts. As Isaac Newton in his *Observations on the Prophecies of Daniel* (1732) put it: "The Book of Daniel is a collection of papers written at several times. The last six chapters contain Prophecies . . . written by Daniel himself." The first six chapters are "a collection of historical papers written by other authors." In the stories about him, written in the third person, Daniel, like the biblical Joseph, is minister to pagan kings and interpreter of signs vouchsafed to them. In the second part, written in the first person, Daniel, like biblical prophets, records signs seen by himself and he is unable to understand their meaning. Now he himself needs an angelic interpreter.

The contrast between the wizard of the narratives and the passive medium of the visions makes it impossible to believe that the stories and the revelations were composed by the same writer. The author of the visions, as we shall see presently, wrote at the time of Antiochus IV Epiphanes (176–164 B.C.E.). But he spoke in the name of Daniel who was already known to readers from the stories which glorified the wisdom of the ancient seer.

Accordingly, this essay is divided in two parts: the first concerns the narratives about Daniel, the second deals with Daniel's visions.

The cylinder seal of King Darius, in the British Museum.
The lion is "set up on feet like a man."

Adelfia's sarcophagus (Christian period). National Museum, Syracuse, Sicily. Among biblical incidents depicted are the Three Youths (lower left), Abraham and Isaac (upper right, next to medallion), and Adam and Eve.

Detail from Adelfia's sarcophagus. The Three Youths defy the command to worship the idol, here represented as a Roman bust.

Daniel, naked and with attendant lions, receives food from the prophet Habakkuk (according to an apocryphal addition in Greek and Latin Bibles). Noah with a bird completes the composition. Relief in Lateran Museum.

Carving on the lid of a sarcophagus. Lateran Museum,
Rome. As an executioner adds fuel to the fiery furnace,
the Three Youths pray (their prayer is an apocryphal addition to the Daniel story in Greek and Latin Bibles).
Left: Noah receiving the returning dove during the flood.

The Narratives

The collection of narratives about Daniel in the Bible, besides a biographical introduction (ch. 1) which we shall examine presently, contains two examples of the miraculous intervention of God (ch. 3, 6) and three stories proving Daniel's superior wisdom (ch. 2, 4, 5). Thus, Daniel of the book like Daniel of Ezekiel is both righteous man and wizard.

FOUR KINGS (DANIEL 2)

The tale of Daniel's wizardry that established his reputation is known to everybody (ch. 2). Nebuchadnezzar calls his diviners to explain his dream, but does not tell it. Dreams remain effective even if the dreamer cannot remember them. The later rabbis composed a prayer supplicating God to turn a forgotten dream into something good for the dreamer. In the story the motif is used to manifest Daniel's unparalleled ability. The wise men of Babylon were unable to discover the forgotten dream. To Daniel the mystery was revealed in a vision. As the rabbis noted, Nebuchadnezzar (and the reader) now cannot doubt Daniel's interpretation. The king saw a colossus, the head of which was of gold, the breast and arms were of silver, the belly and thighs of bronze, and the legs of iron. A stone "cut out by no human hand" smote the image to pieces, became a great mountain and filled the whole earth.

According to the present text, Daniel explains that there would be four kingdoms (gold, silver, bronze, iron), the first the Babylonian empire, then three other ones, until God would set up his own kingdom forever. But this interpretation cannot be the original one. Nebuchadnezzar cannot dream of the Greeks or Romans who do not concern him. One statue cannot be the symbol of four different empires. An empire which overcomes its predecessor must be more powerful. In the ancient Near East a ruler took the title of the universal monarch after defeating the previous champion. But in the vision, as ancient commentators noted, the order of metals is of decreasing value, from gold to iron.

In fact, the dream and its interpretation originally concerned Nebuchadnezzar himself—"you, O King, are the head of gold"—and his heirs in Babylon. Daniel must have announced that the King will have three, and only three, successors. When the Persian Shah Ala-ed-Din Mohammed (1199–1220) saw himself in a dream as having a head of gold, and other parts of the body made of silver, bronze, lead, and tin, his vision indicated that he would have only four successors of his family.

A similar story made Nebuchadnezzar himself predict the fall of Babylon. "A Persian mule" (Cyrus was half-Persian, half-Mede) would come, aided and abetted by Babylonian gods, and bring slavery upon Babylon. Josephus tells that Isaiah's prophecy of Cyrus (Isa. 45) was read to the Persian conqueror. Cyrus mounted a propaganda campaign against Nabonidus, the last king of Babylon. Daniel's oracle was fitted into this propaganda context, if not invented for this purpose.

As a matter of fact, according to history not three but four kings reigned after Nebuchadnezzar in Babylon. But one of these three was an infant assassinated after nine months of reign, and Nabonidus, his successor, proclaimed that the minor had been made king "against the intentions of the gods." Nabonidus' mother accordingly counted in her inscription only two rulers between Nebuchadnezzar and her son. However, the number—whether actual or official—of the kings after Nebuchadnezzar was irrelevant for the success of the prediction concerning the fall of Babylon. "Three" generations was a conventional number for such oracles. A magician told the Pharaoh Cheops, builder of the Great Pyramid, that after the reign of his grandson the royal dignity would pass to another dynasty. In fact, Cheops was followed by four members of his own family. Jeremiah announced (27:6) that all nations shall serve Nebuchadnezzar, his son, and his grandson "until the time of his own land come." In fact, Evil-Merodach, Nebuchadnezzar's son, was assassinated, and was succeeded by a son-in-law of Nebuchadnezzar. In the Second Book of Chronicles (36:21) Jeremiah's prophecy of seventy years of desolation for Jerusalem (29:10) is said to have been fulfilled in the Persian conquest of Babylon. Yet, less than fifty years passed between the Exile (587) and the Return (539). But a fulfilled prediction is not re-checked with the help of chronological tables. A prophecy, uttered or said to have been spoken in the second year of Nebuchadnezzar's dominion over Jerusalem (586), that after three reigns more the Babylonian kingdom would be overthrown, comforted the victims of the "splendor and pride of the Chaldeans" (Isa. 13:19).

We do not know whether the story that foretold the fall of Babylon was of Jewish or of Gentile origin. The redactor of the narrative cycle tells us (Dan. 1:7) that at the court Daniel received the Babylonian name of Belteshazzar. The situation is borrowed from the biblical story of Joseph (Gen. 41:45). But the name of the soothsayer in the original prediction to Nebuchadnezzar, perhaps, was Belteshazzar. In this case, a Jewish editor of the text identified the Babylonian soothsayer with Daniel, a revealer of secrets. The essential fact was that the prophecy of Daniel-Belteshazzar had been fulfilled. The first readers of his prediction could witness the fall of Babylon (539 B.C.E.) forty-seven years after the destruction of Jerusalem (586 B.C.E.). The kingdom of God, it is true, was not established as yet, but Jerusalem was restored and God's people were permitted to return to the holy city. The success of the prediction secured its preservation.

Unfulfilled prophecies are easily forgotten. The favorable oracle received by Nabonidus, the last Babylonian king, and proved false by the event, fell into oblivion for twenty-five centuries until the stone on which it had been hopefully recorded by Nabonidus was recovered by modern archeologists. But the alleged prediction of Nebuchadnezzar announcing the fall of his empire was still known to the Babylonian historian Berossus who wrote in Greek c. 280 B.C.E. Likewise, Daniel's prophecy, written in Aramaic, the common language of the Levant, continued to be copied in Jerusalem and read under the Persian and Macedonian rulers. The interest of later Jewish readers in Daniel's fulfilled prediction was not at all antiquarian. In the Jewish view, Babylon, the first heathen power to conquer Jerusalem, was the prototype of the world empires which, ever since the conquest of Jerusalem by Nebuchadnezzar, had lorded it over God's special people. When the author of Revelations (17:5) wanted to curse Rome under Nero, he called the imperial city "Babylon the great, mother of harlots and of earth's abominations." In the Persian, Greek, and Roman ages the Jews eagerly read, invented, and repeated tales in which a pious and sage Jew and his Deity were shown as superior to the idols and kings of Babylon and thus, by implication, to the present heathen masters of Jerusalem. Accordingly, toward the end of the fourth century B.C.E. a Jewish editor modernized the ancient prophecy of Daniel. He did it because he was influenced by a Persian political theory and because the events seemed to show that Daniel had in mind the new empires and not the long forgotten Babylonian kings.

FOUR EMPIRES (DANIEL 2)

The Persians were upstarts, nomads who happened to conquer the civilized countries of the Near East. The Persian kings were anxious to make themselves equal to the ancient overlords of the Levant. They asserted that the Assyrians were the first race to dominate the world. Nabonidus, the last king of Babylon, pretended to descend from the Assyrian kings and called himself "king of the universe," the title shunned by his Babylonian predecessors. The Medes succeeded the Assyrians (as a matter of fact, Assyria had been overthrown in 612 by a Medo-Babylonian coalition, but the aid of the Babylonians was conveniently forgotten at the Persian court). The Medes in turn, in 553, submitted to their southern neighbors, led by Cyrus. Thus the Persian kings were the legitimate successors to the universal sovereignty of Assyria. This theory was already known and implicitly disavowed by Herodotus, the Greek historian writing in the third quarter of the fifth century, and was expounded some fifty years later by Ctesias, a Greek writer who used Persian sources and represented the Persian world-view. According to him the first Assyrian king, Ninus, and his wife Semiramis already held a world empire which extended from India to Ethiopia—that is, the territories later ruled by the Persian kings. The theory implied that the Persian empire is the lasting one. The Achaemenid dynasty of Darius, whose legitimacy as Cyrus' heir was somewhat suspect, emphasized the principle of loyalty. The Persian education impressed on children the horror of lying, but in the official language disagreement with the official truth was the lie which makes the subjects rebellious.

The Jews accepted this quietist ideology. When, in 520, after the death of Cyrus' son, Cambyses, the empire seemed to be breaking to pieces, Haggai and Zechariah expected that in a little while the Lord of Hosts would shake the heaven and the earth. Such portentous oracles having been confuted by events, the wisdom was now to acquiesce to the Persian rule. The whole conception of the priestly author who wrote the biblical Chronicles is conditioned by this idea. The union between the altar in Jerusalem and the throne of Susa seems to him to be natural and permanent. The Temple is restored "according to the commandments of the God of Israel, and according to the decree of Cyrus, and Darius, and Artaxerxes, king of Persia." Jerusalem was destroyed because her king rebelled against King Nebuchadnezzar, who had made him swear by God. This is taken from Ezekiel (17:13), but the lesson was addressed to the Chronicler's readers: the Jews who had taken the oath of fidelity to the Persian king.

Alexander's conquest in 333 shattered the placidity of Persian Jerusalem. After all, the Third Empire was not the last one. But if the Third Monarchy was mortal, why should the Fourth pagan rule be everlasting? In fact, after Alexander's death in 323 his generals began the internecine war which continued for twenty years. In these twenty years Jerusalem changed her masters seven times. On one occasion, the city was resisting Ptolemy, the Macedonian satrap of Egypt, and fell on a Sabbath. The Jews abstained from fight, only praying with outstretched hands to Heaven. The new and "harsh master" carried away a large number of prisoners as slaves, and others were compelled to settle in Egypt. The operations of other war lords produced similar effects. Besides pillage and capture of towns, each war lord exacted money and supplies. On practically permanent footing, these armed hordes, which included women, children, and slaves of soldiers, traffickers of all kind, and endless baggage-trains, lived well off the country. In 306 an army of eighty thousand foot soldiers and eight thousand horsemen marched through Palestine toward Egypt. After Alexander's death, the nominal kings were his baby son and a simpleton, Alexander's half-brother. Both were murdered by rival war lords, and the whole family of Alexander, from his mother to his sisters and wives, lost their lives in the same way. From 306 on, the war lords abandoned the pretense of fighting for the legitimate kings, and one after another proclaimed himself to be king in his own right. The Fourth Empire went to pieces.

At this time of troubles and despair a sage of Jerusalem elicited the secret of events and the promise of a new age about to dawn, from the old oracle of Daniel. The ancient seer, he believed, spoke not of four kings, but of four kingships. The simile of four metals often illustrated the succession of historical periods. The Greek poet Hesiod, in the eighth century B.C.E., complained that the golden age had been at the beginning and that men now lived in the dreadful age of iron and violence. The new interpreter of Nebuchadnezzar's dream applied the simile to the four universal monarchies. (He may have known the Iranian idea that the divine genius of military power was the patron of metals.) For a Jew, however, not Assyria but Babylon of Nebuchadnezzar, the conqueror of Jerusalem, must have been the first world's lordship. Thus, in the Jewish schema, the four empires were Babylonia, Media, Persia, and Macedonia. But the Jews were not interested in past sovereignties for the sake of history. They did not ask and did not need to inquire whether the Babylonian dominion could be symbolized by gold, the Median by silver, and the Persian by bronze. They knew absolutely that they lived in the dreadful age of iron and violence. But they also clearly saw the approaching end of this age.

In Nebuchadnezzar's dream the feet of the colossus were partly of iron and partly of clay. Similarly, in the story of Bel and Daniel (which has been preserved in Greek) the idol was of bronze without and of clay within. These details were no arbitrary inventions. To cast a metal statue a clay core was needed. The clay was then removed. But in order to stabilize very massive hollow metal pieces or their appurtenances, such as the legs of Nebuchadnezzar's colossus, on completion the clay cores were sometimes retained.

To men who were witnesses and victims of the internecine struggle for Alexander's succession between 321 and 301 it appeared clear that the Fourth Empire was made of "clay and iron." Alexander's universal monarchy now became "the divided kingship." "In the days of those kings" the stone "cut out by no human hand" would smite the heathen dominion forever. God's own kingship over Israel was in sight.

Such adaptation of an ancient oracle may seem strange to us for whom printing machines produce identical exemplars of a text. But Daniel's prophecy circulated only in handmade copies which were often faulty and which, at least in details, almost always disagreed. A man reading between 320 and 300 an old papyrus of Daniel's oracle, the writing now faded, now corrected between the lines, could easily convince himself that the text had been corrupted in the course of time, and that the ancient seer had in mind the present age of the new interpreter. There was an oracle predicting that with the Dorian (Spartan) war a calamity would come to Athens. The calamity was to be *loimos* (plague) or, as others read the prophecy, *limos* (famine). When in 430, during the war against Sparta, a plague struck Athens, the first version became accepted, the people making the meaning of the prophecy fit in with their own experience. Thucydides adds that should another Dorian war ever happen and be accompanied by famine, the verse would be re-interpreted accordingly.

The Egyptian prophecy of the "impure" coming to desecrate the temples of the gods, already known in the second millennium B.C.E., was readapted again and again to mark the new enemies of the holy people on the Nile. One version, which may have originated in the time of Alexander's successors, identified the Greeks with the enemies of the gods, and predicted the destruction of Alexandria. Another Egyptian prophecy, which originally concerned the Persian enemy, was adjusted, probably after Alexander's death, to a new situation. A savior coming from the city of Herakleopolis was again promised. But this time his coming was placed "after the Persians and the Greeks."

The Jewish seer and the Egyptian priests were both soon disappointed. The carnage among the Macedonians ended as suddenly as it had begun. Before and shortly after the battle at Ipsus (301) the confusion had reached its peak. When Ptolemy once again occupied Palestine after Ipsus, everybody expected that Seleucus of Syria would now begin a war against his ally. But declaring that for friendship's sake he would for the present take no action, Seleucus acquiesced in Ptolemy's gain. A long century of Ptolemaic rule in Palestine began. And the Egyptian priests had to correct the calculations of the end. "It will happen," the new interpretation announced, "that the Ionians shall rule Egypt for a long time."

Composed under Nebuchadnezzar, revised under the successors of Alexander toward the end of the fourth century, the prophecy of Daniel was again adjusted some fifty years later to meet a new international crisis. In 252 Antiochus II of Syria married Berenice, daughter of Ptolemy II of Egypt. The royal union promised to open a new era of peace for Palestine, which had long been a cause of dissension between the kings of Egypt, who possessed the country, and the kings of Syria, who laid claim to it.

But after the death of Antiochus II in 246 his first wife, Laodice, seized the power and, to insure her own children's right to the crown, had Berenice and her infant son killed. Ptolemy III, Berenice's brother, invaded Syria and overran Mesopotamia and nearly all of Asia Minor as well. "He shall enter into the stronghold of the King of the North, and shall prevail" (Dan. 11:8). But a rebellion in Egypt compelled Ptolemy III to abandon his conquests. A peace between Syria and Egypt was concluded in 242.

Thus between 246 and 242 the two heathen kingdoms which contested Palestine were themselves in confusion. A Jewish oracle-monger thought that now the time of deliverance promised by Daniel was really at hand. He readjusted the ancient oracle and republished it. His additions were minimal. He added what are now the verses 41–43 of chapter 2, developing the idea of iron mixed with clay, and understanding the expression as a reference to the "mingling by the seed of men." He adds that this union will not hold together, "just as iron does not mix with clay."

Let us observe again that such harmonizing of political prophecies with new contingencies, far from being exceptional, was practiced again and again, even unto our own days. A patriotic prophecy ascribed to an obscure poet, R. Hammerling, who had died in 1889, was circulated by some Austrian nationalists in 1915. It foretold the coming "Germanic century," and announced such future happenings as the invasion of England and the annexation of Poland by Austria. In 1944, German propaganda again circulated this prophecy, but with changes and additions that agreed with the new situation: for instance the text now alluded to the annexation of Czechoslovakia by Germany.[2]

THE TREE OF LIFE (DANIEL 4)

Once the reputation of Daniel as soothsayer was established, his name attracted other stories of forewarning. In one of them (ch. 4) Daniel is again shown in the role of interpreter of dreams. This time Nebuchadnezzar dreams of a tall tree in the midst of the earth. The top of the tree reaches the sky, the beasts of the field find shade under it, and the birds dwell in its branches. An angelic being coming down from heaven proclaims the heavenly decree that the tree be hewn down to the stump to teach that "the Most High rules the kingdom of men." In Mesopotamian texts kings (and priests) receive revelatory dreams which bring celestial messages to the royal dreamer. The court texts naturally record only promises and decorously pass over "evil dreams." In the Bible, however, as the rabbis have observed, God, who often speaks directly to Abraham and Abraham's posterity, communicates with Gentile potentates in dream only.[3] These dream messages are sometimes, as in the dream of Abimelech (Gen. 20), direct warnings; sometimes, as in Pharaoh's case, enigmatic dreams in which, as an ancient author says, the meaning of the vision is concealed with strange shapes and requires an interpretation. Such a dream, according to a rabbinic metaphor, is like a sealed letter.[4] Nebuchadnezzar accordingly calls magicians, enchanters, Chaldeans (that is, astrologers), and exorcists. The exorcists and the enchanters could conjure away the evil dreams. The astrologers were needed to explain astral dreams. The first name on the list (*hartumin*) goes back to the Egyptian term for priests who interpreted dreams; the term was known to the authors of Daniel's stories from Joseph's tale in Genesis, but such Egyptian specialists are known to have been at the Assyrian court and were surely employed in Babylonia as well.

All these wizards, however, are unable to understand the meaning of Nebuchadnezzar's vision. Yet, as the church father Hippolytus observed, this vision does not require an interpreter of dreams; its meaning is obvious to everybody. The tree was a common symbol of life and power. In a fragment found among the Dead Sea Scrolls, a soothsayer sees four trees: one is Persia, another Babylon, etc. In later Iranian texts the world order is represented by a tree with its trunk, branches, etc.; four (or seven) branches of a tree symbolize the eons. In a later rewriting of the patriarchal stories of Genesis, Abraham in a dream sees a cedar uprooted and a palm remaining intact. Sarah knows that Abraham is the cedar and she the palm. Describing Nebuchadnezzar's dream our author intentionally uses the imagery of Ezekiel (31), who likens the Pharaoh to the tallest cedar in Lebanon to be cut down by God because of its pride. God, says Ezekiel (17:24), brings down the tall tree and makes high the low one. In his dream Nebuchadnezzar saw the stump being bound with rings of iron and bronze. Such bands encircle the sacred tree on Mesopotamian monuments.

A royal dream, as the ancient interpreters of dreams knew, has a general meaning. Nebuchadnezzar's dream means that he, or his imperial city, will lose the predominance but still remain alive like a stump. The prophecy agreed with the events of 539. In this year Cyrus of Persia conquered Babylon, but the city was not destroyed (as happened in 612 to Assyrian Nineveh, and in 587 to Jerusalem); it remained a prosperous, albeit provincial, center of the Persian realm. If the tree no longer reached the sky, a stump "amid the tender grass of the field" was nourished by "the dew of heaven." Similarly Nabonidus, the last Babylonian king, after being taken prisoner by the Persians was treated gently and appointed governor of Carmania (now Kirman), on the straits of Ormuzd, in southern Iran. Again the proud tree was cut down but not uprooted, and its stump remained alive.

The fall of the arrogant king, who, as his enemies repeated, pretended that he was wise and knew what was hidden, was a natural occasion for inventing all kinds of stories illustrating the truth so dear to the common man, that pride goeth before a fall. Nabonidus, who had obtained the throne by *coup d'état*, was anxious to learn, as he tells the world on a stone, whether longevity and endurance of his rule would be vouchsafed to him. In a dream he received the promise of these boons, and this dream was proved false in 539. There must have been a truthful vision announcing the king's fate. In accordance with the style of revelation addressed to kings, the divine decree was made known in the dream by a celestial being. It is remarkable that the tale turns upon the motif of "jealousy of gods," which is so well known from Greek literature. In Herodotus (7,10), Artabanus, uncle of the Persian king Xerxes, reminds him before his disastrous Greek campaign that the Deity likes to bring low all that is pre-eminent and suffers none to be proud save Himself.

The same motif appears in late Hebrew texts. The King of Babylon (whom the rabbis identified with Nebuchadnezzar) in Isaiah 14 is warned that he is to be cut down to the ground. The Pharoah who says "My Nile is my own" and the ruler of Tyre will be destroyed, "because thou art proud" (Ezek. 28–29). In Daniel 4 the tree which grew and became strong is the king. He is brought low not for any sin or presumption but because he was so high. God, says Artabanus to Xerxes, sends bolts against the animals, the trees, and the buildings which rise above others. The warning dream, refashioned in Daniel 4, may have been an invention of the enemies of Nabonidus, or it may have been fabricated some twenty years after his fall when the Babylonians, successively led in 521 by two men who pretended to be Nabonidus' sons, rebelled against Persia.

MAN-BEAST (DANIEL 4)

Daniel 4 thus has preserved a Babylonian propaganda tale against Nabonidus, composed sometime before 539 or, perhaps, in 521. The original story does not need to be and probably was not of Jewish origin, and Daniel was substituted by a Jewish editor for some Babylonian wizard. The same or a later Jewish editor had also contaminated the original story with another tale. The contamination is evidenced by the fact that in the present text Daniel's interpretation of the dream disagrees with its contents.

When the Pharaoh Tanutamon (663–50) dreams of two serpents, his courtiers immediately recognize that the vision announces his domination of upper and lower Egypt, for snakes were heraldic symbols of these countries. But according to Daniel the tree cut down means that the king for "seven times" would live with the beasts of the field and eat grass like an ox. Such incongruity in an otherwise well constructed story indicated the use of "rudimentary motifs." The author follows a tradition, but he inserts variants borrowed from a parallel tradition since he believes that his story is true and is anxious to give it exactly, or expects his hearers to be startled if the well-known tradition were to be passed over. For instance, in Euripides' *Medea* the sorceress sends two fatal gifts to her rival, a poisoned dress and a diadem, which burn her and Jason to death. The poet juxtaposed two variants of the death of Creusa. In the parable of the Rich Man and Lazarus in the Third Gospel (16), the Rich Man in hell begs that Lazarus be sent to forewarn his brothers: "If some one goes to them from the dead, they will repent." Abraham refuses the request which does not fit the composition of the tale. But in the old Egyptian variant of the same story, a dead man is returned to the earth to preach repentance.[5] Thus, it appears that the author of Daniel 4 likewise combined two different tales, both of which dealt with the theme that when pride comes, then comes disgrace (Prov. 11:12), and both may have originally concerned Nabonidus.

The last king of Babylon placed his own god, the moon-god Sin, "the King of the gods," above Marduk, the celestial patron of Babylon. As the terrestrial order reflected the hierarchy above, this meant the elevation of Haran, the city of Sin on an affluent of the upper Euphrates, over Babylon. Nabonidus' mother, a devotee of Sin, went clothed in rags for many years, praying to her god (and her goddess, Sin's spouse) for the glory of Haran and the divinities of this city. In early Mohammedan times the population of Haran continued to worship Sin. Like the Jews, the people of Haran prayed for the restitution of their former glory.[6] Disliked by the clergy of Marduk, Nabonidus quarreled with the Babylonians who "like a dog devoured one another." Nebuchadnezzar said in one of his inscriptions that he did not like to live elsewhere than in Babylon and for this reason did not build palaces elsewhere. Nabonidus, as he says himself, went afar "from my city of Babylon," built a palace in Teima, a city of Sin in Arabia, and spent ten years out of the seventeen of his reign in Arabia, "and to my city of Babylon, I did not go," as he tells us.

No wonder the gossipers in Babylon ascribed his absence to some loathsome disease. Among the Dead Sea Scrolls there is the beginning of the "Prayer of Nabonidus," in which the king tells that for seven years of his stay in Arabia, he suffered from *shechin* (the same disease that afflicted Job "from the sole of his foot to the crown of his head"). He was saved by a Jewish exorcist (whose name is not given in the fragment), who advised the king to abandon the worship of idols and to trust in God. The exorcist sent his prescription in writing (a chronically sick king was isolated). When King Uzziah of Judah became proud, he was struck with leprosy and had to dwell in a separate house to the day of his death while his son took over the government (II Chr. 26:16). In his prediction of the fall of Babylon, Nebuchadnezzar curses Nabonidus: might he be drowned in the sea or driven into the desert wandering alone "where wild beasts have their pasture, and birds do roam." The curse spoken by Nebuchadnezzar in Daniel 4 and the "Prayer of Nabonidus" have this trait in common: the arrogant king is excluded from human society; either as an outlaw or as physically or mentally sick he must dwell "where is no city, nor track of man," and with beasts as his sole companions.

The schema of the tale used in Daniel 4 was, it seems, as follows: the king receives advice from above (perhaps in a dream) to break off his sin and practice righteousness. A year later, looking at his city, he boasts (as Nebuchadnezzar does in his inscriptions) that he has built this great Babylon by his power and for his glory. He immediately becomes like a beast until he has learned his lesson, humbles himself, and becomes re-established in his kingdom. The anecdote rationalizes the fairy tale theme of a man transformed into an animal. As the rabbis said, Nebuchadnezzar pretended to be more than a man, and he became a beast.

The story is different from that of the vision of the tall tree. The threatened evil is avoidable. Daniel is not only an interpreter of dreams but one who warns the king. He plays the same role as the prophets of doom in Israel, or the warning counselor of a king in Herodotus and oriental literature.

The madness incident could be grafted on to the tree-story because of the imagery of the latter. The animals who have dwelt in the shadow of the leaves of the tree (cf. Ezek. 17:23) flee from under it when its branches are cut off. But the lot of the low stump is to be with the animals in the grass of the earth. Since the gender of "tree" is masculine in Semitic languages and since the belief in the existence of the tree-spirit is common, the heavenly order, "Let his heart be changed from a man's to that of an animal," could not startle the reader.

In Jewish tradition the mad king of the Babylonian legend became identified with Nebuchadnezzar; the conqueror of Jerusalem, who burned the Temple, was a prototype of arrogance. The Jewish listeners were happy to learn that the proud conqueror had to recognize and proclaim the glory of the Most High, whose dominion "is an everlasting dominion" (Dan. 4:31).

THE WRITING ON THE WALL
(DANIEL 5)

The third story, in which Daniel explains the signs of divine displeasure to a Babylonian king, concerns Belshazzar. Belshazzar was a son of the last Babylonian king Nabonidus. In 553 Nabonidus invested his son with viceroyalty and while the king himself stayed in Arabia (above p. 76), Belshazzar governed Babylon. Nabonidus returned to the capital only in the spring of 539, obviously alarmed by the advance of the Persians, who captured Babylon about six months later. Thus, it is understandable that Belshazzar could be remembered as the last king of Babylon in the popular tradition of Babylonian Jews. A second element that points to the Babylonian origin of the story narrated in Daniel 6 is the idea of its author that Belshazzar was a son of Nebuchadnezzar. Herodotus, who depended on the oral Babylonian tradition, also believed that the last king of Babylon, whom he rightly calls Labinetos (Nabinetos, that is, Nabonidus) was a son of King Labinetos, who according to another passage of Herodotus is to be identified with Nebuchadnezzar. In the prediction of Nebuchadnezzar, Nabonidus is described as an offspring of "a Median woman." In fact, Nabonidus' mother was a very pious lady from the Mesopotamian city Haran. But Nebuchadnezzar himself had a Median wife for whom he built the famous Hanging Gardens of Babylon. Thus, it appears that the popular Babylonian tradition, followed in Daniel 6, made the last Babylonan king a son of the great Nebuchadnezzar.

It was almost inevitable that Daniel, who had predicted the end of the Babylonian empire to the great king Nebuchadnezzar, would be called to repeat the warning to the last Babylonian ruler. The episode is well known. Great masters painted it and poets such as Byron and Heine paraphrased the tale in verse. In the midst of a revel, being in his cups, Belshazzar orders the vessels of Solomon's Temple brought. Josephus supposes that these sacred objects, carried away by Nebuchadnezzar, were deposited in a Babylonian temple. Following the hint of Josephus, the church fathers Jerome and Theodoret of Cyrrhus explain that as long as these vessels continued to be consecrated to divine worship, even the depraved one of idolaters, God was not moved to wrath; but Belshazzar dared to degrade the holy objects by profane use at his feast. Desecration was of course always a hideous crime. In the Sumerian poem on the fall of the city of Agade, the king Naramsin is blamed for various transgressions; among them the author mentions the desecration of the holy vessels of Enlil's temple in Nippur.

Belshazzar suddenly saw the fingers writing on the wall before him, but neither he nor his wise men could read the script. The rabbis concluded it was written in cipher and tried to guess the code. But it is insight and not technical knowledge that was lacking to the Chaldean wizards, who, as Isaiah says (Isa. 47:10), were led astray by their wisdom.

> And Babel's men of age
> Are wise and deep in lore;
> But now they were not sage,
> They saw, but knew no more.

But Daniel, as Byron says, "saw that writing's truth." Josephus and then the church father Hippolytus believed that the pagan soothsayers could not find out the meaning of "God's characters." This agrees with the generally popular idea that spirits have their own kind of writing. But the inspired Daniel could read and understand it. "And this is the writing that was inscribed: *Mn mn tkl uprsin.*" The words seem to give a descending series of weights: mina (100 shekels), shekel, and two divisionary units (*prs:* divide, a part). This was probably some proverbial locution. The rabbis could say of the eminent son of a less distinguished father: "mina, son of a half of a mina." The formula perhaps referred originally to four Babylonian rulers: Nebuchadnezzar, Neriglissar, his son-in-law, and the pair Nabonidus and Belshazzar. Daniel, however, reads the words as passive verbs and gives the interpretation: "God has numbered thy kingdom, weighed art thou and found wanting, thy kingdom is divided and given to the Medes and the Persians." "In that very night the Chaldean king was slain and Darius the Mede received the kingdom." The Jewish author shifted the emphasis "from the cleverness of the interpreter to the justice of God." [7] The divine weighing decides the balance of history. In fact, Daniel's speech to Belshazzar is a sermon on the danger of pride, the topic that the speaker illustrates by the examples of Nebuchadnezzar and Belshazzar. As the church father John Chrysostom finely observed, Daniel's words can be of no use for Belshazzar whose fate has already been fixed. Belshazzar was not called to humble himself and be saved (as Daniel advises Nebuchadnezzar in ch. 4). Daniel rather speaks to make his readers better: his address, says Chrysostom, belongs to the "advisory" class of speeches. The use of the divine title "the Most High" and the quotations from chapter 4 of Daniel prove that chapter 5 was not set down before the second part of the third century B.C.E. The dating of this chapter is important because it offers the earliest example of the kind of interpretation that later became enormously popular among the Jews.

Daniel says to the king: I shall make known the

pesher. The term appears very often (thirty-two times) in Daniel. It means "interpretation." Koheleth (8:1) can ask: "Who knows the interpretation (*pesher*) of this word?" In connection with dreams, the term *pisru, pasaru*, meaning "solve," was already used in Akkadian. As *patar* it appears in Joseph's story (Gen. 40–41). In all of these passages the term refers to the explanation of some enigma: Joseph explains Pharaoh's dream of seven good and seven lean cows. But in Belshazzar's story, *pesher* for the first time in extant Jewish tradition opposes the plain and the secret meaning of a text. Joseph says that seven lean cows symbolize seven years of hunger. Daniel does not say what mina or shekel signify to the king. He substitutes for these words new ones: *mene, tekel, peres* (not *parsin* as in the inscription he has to explain) and goes on from this new text. Later, in Daniel 9, seventy years of desolation of Jerusalem predicted by Jeremiah become seventy weeks of years. About a century later, in the commentary on Habakkuk found among the Dead Sea Scrolls, when the prophet speaks of sacrifices to the net (1:16), the *pesher* is: the sacrifices to the (Roman) standards.

The text appears to its interpreter as ciphered. Habakkuk (1:6) speaks of the *Casdim*. For the interpreter they are not the Chaldeans of the times of Habakkuk, but the "*Kittim*" (the Romans) of his own time. The same method was used in late Egyptian and Babylonian texts. In the latter ancient geographical names mentioned in prognostications of the future received contemporary identifications. In the Egyptian priestly decree of 198 B.C.E., preserved on the Rosetta stone, the traditional Egyptian emblems of the serpent and the vulture "indicate" that King Ptolemy V "illuminates" Egypt. The method demanded atomization of the oracular text. As Daniel does before Belshazzar, every word must or may be explained separately. The New Testament writers, the rabbis, and the church fathers applied the same method to biblical texts, which were treated as if they were reports of *omina* or dreams. No wonder the haggadists borrowed the rules of interpretation from dream books.[8]

THE LIONS' DEN (DANIEL 6)

To these three examples of Daniel's wizardry the compiler added two tales showing how God saves His servants. King Darius intended to make Daniel his vizir. To trip Daniel up, the courtiers persuaded Darius to forbid petitions to any deity or man except the king for thirty days. Daniel, however, continued to pray three times daily, going on his knees and uttering "petitions and praises" to God. Likewise the Psalmist (55:18) voices his complaints to God "evening and morning and at noon." Daniel is denounced by the courtiers and thrown into the lions' den, but is found unhurt next morning. According to the principle of retribution, his accusers in turn are thrown to the same lions, and devoured "before they reached the bottom of the pit."[9]

The tale touched the heart of readers for more than two thousand years. In I Maccabees (2:60), toward the end of the second century B.C.E., and soon afterwards in III Maccabees, Daniel delivered from the mouth of the lions exemplifies the truth that God saves the innocent man. The art of the Synagogue and then of the Church glorifies Daniel standing victoriously between two lions.

Yet the royal edict which is the starting point of the so popular tale appears absurd to the modern reader and it already perplexed the pious souls of former times. Theodoret of Cyrrhus, who died c. 400, in his commentary on Daniel asks who could be so unreasonable as to imagine that the king may give health, life, children, or rain—the common requests of man imploring the heavens. Accordingly, six centuries before Theodoret, the Greek translator of Daniel had transformed the tale into an attack against ruler-worship: Darius forbids addressing requests to any god but himself.

The story, however, takes place in Babylonia, and the Babylonians were obsessed by the fear of unlucky days: if a man digs a well in the month of Tammuz, his wife will die. The same superstition influenced the religious calendar of the Babylonians. On five days of every month, nobody was to consult a seer. The king was warned not to pray to gods Sin and Shamash (Moon and Sun) on five different days of the month of Nisan, or to his personal god on the fifteenth and thirtieth days of Nisan. Penitential prayers were banned during five months out of twelve; food offerings (and thus the accompanying request) to one's personal god would be unlucky in the month of Tebet. Certain rites could not be performed during the three summer months and also in Kislev and Tebet.

Though Babylonian (and Jewish) months were lunar, now of 29, now of 30 days, Babylonian lists of lucky and unlucky days count thirty days for any month. This explains the interdiction of requests during thirty days in Daniel. The Jewish tale-teller misunderstood the Babylonian ritual, and imagined that during this period no request to a god or a man was allowed. In the same manner the Greeks and Romans, including the Emperor Augustus, believed and through centuries repeated that the Sabbath, on which the Jews did not cook, was a sad day of fasting.

The Jewish author used the misunderstood trait of the Babylonian religion for his edifying purpose. Daniel

6 is essentially a variation on a common theme of oriental folk tales: a virtuous minister is falsely accused and his innocence is proved. The Aramaic story of Achiqar of the same type was already known to Jews at Elephantine in the fifth century B.C.E. Writing for Jewish readers, the author of Daniel 6 wanted to introduce something touching them directly in the Oriental court story. In the same manner modern novels about the first Christians cannot avoid picturing the hero as the martyr of his faith.

The difficulty for the author of Daniel 6 was that until his time, at least, the Jews had never been persecuted for their faith. He had heard, however, that the Babylonians, in their superstitious absurdity, had banned prayers during an unlucky month. But Daniel's and the reader's God always accepted petitions. The theme of the religious conflict between the true faith and heathenism was now easy to elaborate, and the triumphal end was obvious. Darius not only acquits Daniel, he also orders that all men in his dominion should tremble and fear before the God of Daniel.

Yet, rereading the story attentively, we discover threads which show that the Jewish novelist used and contaminated various sources. First, we note the strange trait that only petitions to the king were allowed during the month of prohibition of prayers. In the present text the detail is irrelevant. But here again we have a "rudimentary" motif, a relic of a lost version, in which the minister (or someone on his behalf) had recourse to the king. The envious courtiers, however, confronted the king with "the law of the Medes and Persians" that a royal ordinance may not be frustrated even by the king himself.

This hypothetical reconstruction is confirmed by

the central episode of the tale: cast into the lions' den, Daniel is subjected to a legal ordeal.

The ordeal as a test of innocence was well known to the ancient peoples, including the Babylonians and the Jews. The use of wild animals in this trial does not seem to be attested in the ancient world, but lions are more impressive in a story than would be, say, the Babylonian test of a man denounced for witchcraft: he was acquitted if he did not go down in the river. There was recourse to the ordeal when there was no direct evidence of guilt. In Mosaic law (Lev. 20:10), adultery was punished with death. But a woman suspected of misconduct, if there was no witness of it, was tested by having her drink the "bitter water," which swelled the guilty body.

Daniel's disobedience, however, was witnessed by his accusers. He performed his prayers openly before windows of his upper chamber facing Jerusalem. The ordeal was superfluous in his case. In fact, the function of ordeal here is not to test whether the accused did commit the imputed crime but to determine whether his action was of the nature of crime. Darius sets his heart to deliver Daniel (6:15). The king, as Theodotion says, became not Daniel's judge but his advocate. Unable to save Daniel by his own decree, he appeals to the heavens. As Jerome says: "What he could not obtain by himself, he transferred to the power of God."

The deity was of course the supreme judge of right and wrong. As a Babylonian text says of god Shamash (the Sun god): he reinstates the right of him who has been badly treated. The contest is no longer between Daniel and his accusers: he remains passive. In the fasting prayer of the Synagogue God is supplicated to hear the worshipers as He had responded to Daniel while he was in the lions' den. But later interpreters add something here that is not in the text and that disagrees with the structure of Daniel 6. It is the king and not Daniel who expresses (6:17) the conviction that God will deliver His servant. The contest is now between Darius and his lords. The pit of the lions is sealed by the signets of the king and of his grandees to prevent either party in the conflict from tampering with the test. Daniel passes it unhurt, and, having been found "innocent" by God, he could have done no wrong to the king either (6:23).

The postulate of the story is the same as in folklore: a miraculous happening at an execution (the rope at the gallows breaks, and so on) proves the innocence of the accused. But this time the miracle also and above all manifests the truth of the Jewish faith. We are reminded of the contest between Elijah and the prophets of Baal, where the test of fire revealed the might of the Lord (I Kings 18). The God of Daniel, as King Darius proclaims, "works signs and wonders in heaven and on earth" (6:28).

THE TEST OF TRUTH (DANIEL 3)

God also saves His servants in the story of the Three Youths, in which Daniel is not even mentioned. It was included by the compiler of the Daniel cycle because it paralleled the tale of Daniel in the den of the lions.

Nebuchadnezzar sets up a golden colossus "in the plain of Dura, in the province of Babylon." To this state pageant he commands "all the rulers of the provinces," among them Shadrach, Meshach, and Abednego, the three companions of Daniel, who on his request had been appointed "to administer the province of Babylon" (2:49) as his deputies. Daniel himself was governor of the whole province of Babylonia and "chief overseer of all the wise men in Babylon." Thus, his duties kept him in the capital "at the gate of the king" (2:49), and he did not come to the plain of Dura.[10] (The rabbis, who did not always realize how carefully the compiler of the book planned the story of Daniel, gratuitously supposed that the prophet was sent away from the country by the king.)

At a signal all present at the dedication ceremony fall down and worship the idol, save the three Jewish youths. Accused by informers, they are thrown into the burning furnace, but the fire has no power over their bodies, and Nebuchadnezzar acknowledges the power of the God of the three youths.

The refusal to bow before an idol was a good theme of edifying literature. But the tale of the three youths is the earliest extant specimen of the literary handling of this theme.

Nebuchadnezzar could say to the confessors, as he did according to the rabbis: when you were in your own land, you did worship the idols.[11] From Solomon to Josiah the idols of Astarte, Chemosh, and Milkom were worshiped by the people of the Lord (II Kings 23:13), and there were no Jewish martyrs. It is true that from Hur, in the times of Moses and Aaron, to Zechariah under the King Joash and Uriah the son of Shemiah, a contemporary of Jeremiah, the government or the people persecuted the prophets of the Lord, who preached against idolatry. Jerusalem was the city that killed the prophets and stoned those who were sent to it (Matt. 23:37). But they were stoned because they spoke against the city and against the land (Jer. 26:20), invoking God's wrath on the unfaithful Israel: "You have forsaken the Lord, He has forsaken you" (II Chron. 24:20). According to a Jewish legend already told in the second century B.C.E., Jeremiah found the Jews sacrificing to a golden

image of Baal. He upbraided the people, and king Jehoiakim burned him alive. But the king did not try to
compel the prophet to worship the idol. In polytheism
it was anyone's privilege to partake in blessings vouchsafed by a deity. A stranger sojourning among the Hebrews was allowed, if he wished, to offer a sacrifice to
the Lord (Num. 15:14). Nobody demanded from a Jew
in Babylonia or Egypt that he worship the local gods.
It would be natural, however, for a foreigner to seek the
protection of the deities of the land of his sojourn. The
rabbis made Nebuchadnezzar quote Deuteronomy (4:27–
28) to the three youths: the Lord will scatter you among
the peoples, and there you will serve gods of wood and
stone.

The conflict between the monotheistic Jew and the
alien worshiper could arise only when a Jew became an
officer of a foreign ruler. Every king was also head of the
state religion, and every official action had its religious
aspect. Naaman, general of Ben-Hadad, king of Damascus in the middle of the ninth century, was healed by
the prophet Elisha and he promised to sacrifice to no
deity but the Lord. But when his master entered the
temple of Rimmon with him, he also had to bow before
the idol (II Kings 5:18).

Jewish officers of Persian and Macedonian kings likewise had to be present very often at idolatrous ceremonies. The Persian magi, like the Jews, condemned idolatry, and Herodotus tells us that the Persians had no idols
and regarded the worship of images as foolish. But Artaxerxes II (404–359) set up statues of the goddess Anahita in her temples. Nehemiah was a trusted courtier of
Artaxerxes I. What did a Jew in the position of Nehemiah
under Artaxerxes II have to do when his king made
obeisance to a statue of the goddess? A Jewish courtier
who would dare to offend the Persian king by refusing

to revere "thy gods" (3:18), as the three youths did, would surely make his master "furious" (3:19) and would in all probability be sent to the gallows without much ado. The Macedonian king would be less irate in a similar situation, but, as in the story of Bel (which has been preserved in the Greek Bible), he surely would ask Daniel: Why do not you bow to Bel? The execution or even the simple dismissal of the recalcitrant Jewish officer would prove to the court that the God of the Jews is powerless or at least does not care to protect His confessors. The church father Hippolytus who commented on the tale, c. 204 C.E., when the Christians were persecuted, formulates this dilemma: if God does not save His confessors, the infidels will reprove Him. If He saves all who are persecuted, there will be no martyrs to testify to the faith. Thus, He delivers only a few.

The story of the three youths was written to silence the critics of Providence. The confessors are here thrown into the fiery furnace. Why does the king choose this mode of execution? The disobedient servants of the king could as well be impaled or beheaded, and so on. Nebuchadnezzar explains his order. Like Sennacherib demanding the surrender of Jerusalem (Isa. 37:10), the king asks the confessors: Who is the god who can deliver you out of my hand? (3:15). The three youths are not punished but put to the test. In Iran, the ordeal of fire could test the truth of a religion and of its preachers. Zoroaster himself was said to have walked on fire to demonstrate the truth of his message.[12] Nebuchadnezzar sees Shadrach, Meshach, and Abednego, who were thrown bound into the exceedingly hot furnace, walking unhurt in the midst of the fire and accompanied by an angel (3:25). The test has proved that their doctrine was just. As Nebuchadnezzar says himself (3:28): they were justified in "counteracting the king's words." The terminology as well as the situation are the same as in the tale of Daniel in the lions' den. But now the contest is not between the king and Daniel's accusers but between a new Sennacherib and the Lord. Accordingly, the three confessors are not passive, as Daniel was in the story of the lions. They do not accept the king's challenge and they refuse to state that God will deliver them. Yet they would not worship the idol (3:18). As Cyprian (who himself was put to death as a Christian martyr in 258) explains: they were ready to die for the sake of God whom they served. Their words and their deed solve in advance the aforementioned dilemma of Hippolytus. God can deliver His confessors, as He does in the case of the three youths. The misbelievers who doubt His power are confounded. Nebuchadnezzar now threatens a death penalty to "any people, nation, or language" who speak of "remissness" (*shalu*) of the God of the three youths, since there is no other god who is able to deliver in this manner (3:29). But even if God does not intervene, the faithful have to refuse the homage to the idols.

The narrator is more intransigent than the prophet Elisha. The rabbis understood the meaning of the tale when they made the three youths say that Nebuchadnezzar was the king in matters of state services and taxes, but if he demanded service to idols, he was a barking dog (here is a wordplay: *nebah*, barking). The pagans could retort, as they did in Asia Minor under Augustus, that if the Jews demanded citizenship rights and thus pretended to be our kinfolk, they should also worship our gods. The Jews likewise required full conversion of men who wanted to enter the ranks of the chosen people. But being monotheists, they measured their true faith and the superstitions of their neighbors by different standards. Their intolerance was a virtue, that of the Gentiles a sin. Two times two makes four. A teacher will not tolerate students who insist that two times two may also be three, or five, and so on. And the mission of Israel was to teach the arithmetic truth of one sole deity to the erring nations of the world.

The story of the three youths is placed by the narrator in the time of the Babylonian king Nebuchadnezzar. But the author uses the Persian motif of fire ordeal, and the transcribed Greek names of musical instruments in 3:5 prove that he wrote after 300 B.C.E. Nebuchadnezzar in recognizing the power of the deity of the three youths calls Him "The Most High God" (3:26,32). This was the official title of the Lord of Jerusalem in the Hellenistic Age. The tale was thus composed in the third century B.C.E. Therefore, it offers the earliest, though as yet only an implicit, statement of the doctrine of separation of Church and State: Render to Caesar the things that are Caesar's and to God the things that are God's (Matt. 22:21).

As a matter of fact, the doctrine of freedom of worship could have been formulated only by a monotheist minority which wanted the privilege of non-participating in the official religion of the state. This doctrine was granted recognition in order to avoid or at least mitigate the collisions between monotheistic sects, each of which pretended to be in possession of the absolute and sole truth. The pagans knew and recognized modestly that there is no exclusive road to the great mystery of the Divinity: *Non posse uno itinere ad tam grande secretum pervenire*. The pagan Symmachus who wrote these words to a Christian emperor in 394 thereby formulated the essence of the ecumenical idea which appears so new and for this reason exciting to the churchmen of today.

The Editor of Daniel's Stories

Daniel's tales, preserved in the Bible, were well known in Jerusalem about 170 B.C.E., as we shall see presently. On the other hand, as we have seen (p. 70). Daniel 2:43 alludes to the marriage between Antiochus II of Syria and the Egyptian princess Berenice in 252 B.C.E. and the war between Syria and Egypt after her death in 246 B.C.E. So the biblical collection of Daniel's stories was made in the second half of the third or in the beginning of the second century B.C.E. Daniel was the hero of many legends. Three of them (Daniel and the idol of Bel, Daniel and the Dragon, Daniel exonerating the chaste Susanna) found their way into the Greek Bible. Among the Dead Sea Scrolls there are fragments of a hitherto unknown revelation ascribed to Daniel.[13] But the compiler of the biblical collection did not know or he disregarded these parallel stories.

The editor made a book out of five disparate tales he offered to the reader. First, a prefatory tale (ch.1) narrates how Daniel and the three youths, carried off with other captives from Jerusalem, were brought up at the court of Nebuchadnezzar. They remained loyal to the faith of their fathers, particularly in the matter of the dietary laws. Thus, the ideological unity of the book is made apparent from the beginning. The collection offers lessons in steadfastness to Jews of the Diaspora who grew up and lived among the Gentiles.

Secondly, the editor gave chronological unity to his book. His schema was explained by Theodoret of Cyrrhus (died c. 460 C.E.) in commentary on Daniel. From Jeremiah (25:1) he knew that the first year of Nebuchadnezzar as the overlord of Jerusalem coincided with the fourth year of Jehoiakim, king of Judah. Therefore, "the princes of Judah" (among them Daniel and his companions) were brought to Babylon (Jer. 24:1) in the third year of Jehoiakim (Dan. 1:1). Two years later, in the second year of Nebuchadnezzar (2:1), Daniel gives his first revelation. On the other hand, Daniel prophesied until the first year of Cyrus (1:21), the date of the return of the Chosen People to their land (II Chr. 36:22). This chronological framework explains the mystery of "Darius the Mede" (6:1), which troubles the commentators of Daniel.

The editor has the tale about Daniel in the den of the lions (Daniel ch. 6) happening under "King Darius." But (Persian) kings of this name all reigned after Cyrus; therefore the king of the tale had to be another Darius who preceded Cyrus. The scheme of four empires (above p. 65) as well as biblical prophecies (Isa. 13:17; Jer. 51:11) demanded that Babylon should be conquered by "the kings of the Medes" (Jer. 51:28). Accordingly, the editor called Darius of the tale "Mede" and had him succeed Belshazzar, the last Babylonian king (6:1), and be succeeded by Cyrus (6:29).

The chronological scheme of the book makes Daniel the prophet of the exile. He speaks in the Diaspora and for its edification. In Jerusalem his religion was solid and uncontested. It was the official religion of Hellenistic Jerusalem, and no other worship was tolerated in Judea under the Macedonian kings.[14] Only flesh of animals traditionally recognized as fit for food and sacrifice was to be consumed in Jerusalem. In the Diaspora, the observ-

ance of food laws was difficult. In the prefatory tale
(1:16) the compiler of Daniel's stories convinces the
reader that for a faithful Jew water and vegetables can
be more nutritious than the rich food from the table of
a pagan king.

Above all, in the Diaspora the God of Jerusalem had
to meet the competition of the idols of the Gentiles, and
many Jews succumbed to the attraction of foreign cults.
We can still read the story of a Jewish slave at Oropus
in Boeotia, inscribed on stone in the first half of the third
century B.C.E.[15] He had a dream that obviously appeared
significant to him. The main shrine of Oropus was of
the god Amphiaraus, famous for the interpretation of
dreams. To receive the oracle, the Jew, like everyone
who consulted Amphiaraus, must have offered a sacrifice
to this Greek deity. The oracle interpreted the dream as
indicating that the Jew would be set free by his master.
This happened and the Jew, according to the instructions
of Amphiaraus and the goddess Hygieia, recorded the
whole episode on a stone at the pagan altar. The priests
at Oropus did not care whether a Jew who came to their
shrine also worshiped the God of Jerusalem.

Polytheism was tolerant by virtue of ignorance: nobody could know and measure the power of any god. For
the same reason, the rivalry of cults was fierce though
rather businesslike. Priests and worshipers asserted that
their own god alone was omnipotent. Such advertising
of a particular god is attested in Egypt as early as the
second millennium B.C.E. The reader of the inscription is
advised "to beware" of the power of the praised deity.
Some twenty centuries later, to quote another example,
the description of a wonder performed by the god Sarapis
of Alexandria is followed by the appeal: "Say, there is
(only) one Zeus Serapis." The competition of gods sometimes led to conflicts between the devotees. The restora-

tion of the temple of Sin in Haran was an act of exalted piety for Nabonidus' mother, a devotee of Sin. For the priests of Marduk in Babylon, the work at Haran was an "abomination." Cyrus, their ally, blamed Nabonidus for not reverencing Marduk, and destroyed the sanctuaries built by him. The Persian king Gaumata destroyed some holy places in Iran which Xerxes then restored. Xerxes himself destroyed a place where "daemons" were worshiped and established there the cult of Ahuramazda and of the Holy Righteousness. In 410, the priests of the Egyptian god Khnum, having obtained the help of the local Persian officer, destroyed the temple of the Lord at Elephantine, burned its furniture, and carried away the utensils.

A minority lost in the immense space of the Persian and then the Seleucid empires, living for generations far away from the seat of its deity, wanted and needed to be reassured of the universal might of the Lord of Jerusalem. The Psalmist (148:11) called on the kings of the earth and all peoples to praise the name of the Lord. The collection of Daniel's tales demonstrated that the kings of the earth recognized the might of the God of Jerusalem. Belshazzar alone, one night, dared to affront the Lord of Zion: "In that very night Belshazzar the Chaldean king was slain" (5:30). In four other stories of Daniel's book the pagan sovereigns, as if following the wish of the Psalmist, abundantly praise the name of the Lord. Nebuchadnezzar (3:29) and Darius the Mede (6:27) also order that "all the peoples, tribes and languages" should respect the God of the three youths and "tremble and fear before the God of Daniel." Thus, the Jews on one hand set at nought the king's command to serve his gods and at the same time expect him to command all his subjects to revere the God of the Jews. But the monotheistic minority, necessarily involved in religious conflicts with their polytheist neighbors, found solace in the stories which demonstrated how the Lord of Jerusalem had compelled the heathen emperors to declare His greatness and to threaten His detractors.

For his purpose, the editor heavily underlined the "Jewishness" of the hero. A competition of soothsayers became a contest between a prophet of God and the Chaldean savants. The chastisement of Nebuchadnezzar taught the principle that "the Most High rules in the kingdom of man." Nebuchadnezzar's vision of the colossus was, as we have seen, modernized, and the editor hoped that God's kingdom would still arise in his time.

This pious hope did not prevent him and his readers from rejoicing in the very secular advancement of Jews at heathen courts. As the unbeliever Porphyry observed acidly, the saintly Daniel climbs up and up in the pagan hierarchy. Porphyry failed to mention that Daniel also became "master of the magicians" (4:6) though the practice of pagan divinations had been repeatedly condemned in the Law and attacked by the prophets of Israel. But it seemed natural to the compiler that children of Israel might be admitted to the wisdom of the Chaldeans (1:4), The term *Casdim* ("Chaldeans" in Greek and then in modern versions) was for him no longer the designation of a people, nor even of the Babylonian priestly caste. As in the contemporary Greek writings, "Chaldeans" meant for him "astrologers," and all wise men of Babylon were included by him under the generic term of "Sages." By his time, Babylonian divination was no longer the closely guarded secret of priestly families. Under the Achaemenid domination, Persian magi at Babylon had learned divination techniques from the native soothsayers. The Babylonian Berossus opened an astrological school on the island of Cos about 280.

Wonderfully written as it was, the Daniel collection

was always read and listened to for sheer pleasure and entertainment. A part of its literary success is due to the Hellenistic taste of the editor. The stories retold in Daniel were originally narrated in the international style of folk tales. Nebuchadnezzar, burner of the Temple and a man of eight sins in the Jewish tradition, is here a standardized king of the Oriental popular stories, from the ancient Egyptian novelettes to the Arabian Nights. He is indistinguishable from Sennacherib in the story of Achiqar or Darius in the same Daniel cycle. Yet the historical Darius restored the Temple of Jerusalem. The conflicts between Daniel and other courtiers are here purely accidental and personal. The contrast is not between Jewish light and pagan darkness, but between the caprices of the foolish khalif and the wits of the hero. Nebuchadnezzar can be as angry at Babylonian diviners (ch. 2) as at Jewish confessors. To be a courtier is a dangerous business in Daniel's tales, but so is it also in Esther and in stories that were told about the ancient pharaohs or about the khalifs of Baghdad.

The readers liked the tales because the subject was so interesting: the boy who, against all odds, by sheer intelligence and moral goodness, like Joseph of old, achieves power, money, and fame. From Joseph in Genesis to Horatio Alger's heroes, this theme of success through virtue fascinated readers, perhaps for the reason that nothing like it was ever seen in real life.

But the compiler made these Oriental court stories even more interesting to the reader by his skill in correlating and at the same time varying his materials. For instance, the vessels of the Temple which were to be misused by Belshazzar in chapter 5 are mentioned in the beginning of the book as having been carried off by Nebuchadnezzar. Daniel's appointment as master of the royal diviners, mentioned at the end of chapter 2, naturally makes him the one to whom appeals are brought in the last resort, when all other specialists have failed, as in chapters 4 and 5.

The editor also excels in the art of variation. In chapter 4 Daniel is summoned by Nebuchadnezzar, but in chapter 5 the queen mother suggests calling him. The change is not arbitrary: Belshazzar, the new king, is supposed to have ignored the visitation of Nebuchadnezzar. Of the two tales about the latter, one (ch. 2) is a historical record, the other (ch. 4) is put into the form of a royal proclamation. Again, Nebuchadnezzar on one occasion demands that his magicians divine his dream (ch. 2) and on another, narrates his night vision (ch. 4). In the first martyrdom story, the king orders the three confessors thrown into the fire (ch. 4), while Darius punishes Daniel reluctantly, in obedience to the royal law (ch. 6). When Daniel's enemies wish to outwit Darius, they address him according to the court etiquette: "King Darius live for ever." But they speak abruptly when denouncing Daniel.

Again, the first revelation to Nebuchadnezzar is narrated as if it were an entry in a chronicle (ch. 2): "In the second year of the reign of Nebuchadnezzar . . . then the king made Daniel great. . . ." But in chapter 4, the event is related in a royal letter.[16] In the last mentioned case we can still see how the compiler worked. Babylonian scribes put their historical—and pious—novelettes into the form of royal inscriptions attributed to some bygone ruler. For instance, Naramsin, a Sumerian king of old, is made to tell that he consulted oracles which announced a horrible invasion. When the enemy came he, obviously against the advice of gods, attacked, was defeated, and then, by following a new heavenly revelation—this time favorable—he succeeded in driving out the invaders. He concludes by advising meekness to his successors. The story in Daniel 4, the Babylonian sources

of which are obvious, has the same style ("I, Nebuchadnezzar . . ."), structure (the king recovers his dominion
by meekly following the heavenly will), and the pious
finale. But the editor not only judaized his model. He
also transformed the inscription, which by definition is a
local record, into an encyclical addressed "to all the peoples, tribes, and languages" on the earth, that is, in the dominion of Nebuchadnezzar (3:31). Darius likewise writes
to "all the peoples, tribes, and languages" to proclaim the
power of the God of Daniel (6:26). The compiler has in
mind circular letters which Hellenistic kings dispatched
to all constituent parts of the realm.[17]

Oriental storytellers liked repetitions and digressions.
Three times Delilah tries to find out Samson's secret.
Even in the stories built in crescendo, such as Joseph and
Tobit, the denouement is intentionally retarded by secondary episodes. This is the international style of folk
tales, common to the Bible and Homer, to ancient Egyptian stories as well as to the Arabian Nights. The author
of Daniel, however, narrated compactly and avoided
digressions. The inability of the Babylonian seers to interpret the dreams is described in the first episode as a
contrast to Daniel's art. Their failure to solve other rid-
dles is afterwards simply stated and not dramatized. In
the first story Daniel prays in order to obtain illumina-
tion. This motif does not appear later. The narrative goes
straight to the climax, and details serve the construction
of plot. If we hear that three youths were thrown into
the furnaces fully clothed, this detail later evidences the
miracle: the garments did not show even the least whiff
of fire and smoke. Explaining the dreadful dream of his
king, Daniel begins with the safeguarding formula: "May
the dream be for thy enemies." This example of courtly
behavior, which the author needed for the sake of local
color, later disturbed rabbinic commentators.

This artistic parsimony, reminiscent of the modern

short story, was characteristic of the Ionian novelistic style. A dream having signified to Croesus that his son Atys will die "by a point of iron," every narrated incident brings the realization of the presage a step nearer. On the other hand, the climax of the story is announced beforehand. Croesus deems himself to be the most fortunate of all men. For that the divine Nemesis falls upon him. The hearer knows in advance that Croesus will not escape retribution and that "the point of iron" will slay his son. Likewise, a prediction interpreted by Daniel cannot but be realized. Whence did both Herodotus and the editor of Daniel derive this literary technique? One wonders whether the tale of divine retribution may not have been the source of the short story.

As a matter of fact, the Babylonian tale of Naramsin (p. 98) shows how a miracle story redacted as a historical record could become the model of the new literary technique. The story is a fictionized account of a remarkable incident and so can imitate the sobriety of a chronicle.

Prophecies and Hindsights

DANIEL'S REVELATIONS

The collection of Daniel tales was published, as we have seen (p. 92), after 245 and probably before 219, when Antiochus III temporarily occupied Ptolemaic Palestine, which he lost two years later. The success of this book renewed the fame of the ancient seer. Its popularity induced the first author (or authors) of Daniel's revelations to choose this pseudonym when he (or they) endeavored to revivify the hopes of God-fearing Jews under the persecution of Antiochus Epiphanes. These Jews felt betrayed by their countrymen who promoted and accepted the religious reform, and feared themselves forgotten by the Lord who tarried in punishing the apostates and in bringing down their royal protector. The prophets of old were of little help; their foreknowledge of the future did not extend beyond the Exile and the restoration, events which to the contemporaries of Epiphanes more than three centuries afterwards appeared as venerable marks of the long forgotten past. But Daniel of the tale-book predicted the Hellenic kingdom, and also its fall and the establishment of the kingdom of God. As Philo says of Moses, the fulfillment of some of his predictions confirms the validity of those which have not yet been realized.

The dependence of Daniel's revelations on Daniel's tales appears clearly in the chronological framework. All revelations happen after Nebuchadnezzar: the imitators did not dare to duplicate the classical prophecy about the succession of empires, announced to Nebuchadnezzar. Two visions (ch. 7, 8) are placed under Belshazzar, the last Babylonian king according to the tales (ch. 5). The vision of chapter 9 is placed under the imaginary Darius the Mede who allegedly became king over the Chaldeans after Belshazzar (6:1). The fourth vision (ch. 10–12) happens under Cyrus the Persian, who, according to the tales-book (6:28) succeeded Darius the Mede.

THE FOUR BEASTS (*DANIEL* 7)

The earliest propaganda tract was the vision of the Four Beasts (ch. 7). As the ancient commentators uniformly noted, this dream of Daniel parallels the dream of Nebuchadnezzar (ch. 2). In our terms this means that the younger writer imitates the older one. For this reason he likewise writes in Aramaic, the language of the tale-book. Besides, in his time Aramaic was the international language by which people throughout the Near East had communicated since the heyday of the Assyrian Empire. At the time of Epiphanes a book written in Aramaic could find readers from Elephantine at the southern frontier of Egypt to Jerusalem, and from Jerusalem to the Himalayan mountains and the Aral sea.

But, imitating Nebuchadnezzar's dream, the new author naturally tries to improve on it. The report in chapter 2 is anonymous; nobody vouches for it. The dream of chapter 7 was written down by Daniel himself. As Jerome observes, the seer alone was aware of his dream, while in Daniel's tales the "barbarous nations" (that is, the Gentiles) were concerned with the seer's revelations. The embroidering of Daniel's dream is also more fanciful than the rather simple pattern of Nebuchadnezzar's dream. Four winds stir the great sea, this symbol of the world, as Jerome says, and four beasts come out from the great sea. The first three are a lion with eagle wings, a bear, and a winged leopard. In Babylonian astral geography lion, bear, and leopard respectively symbolized the south (Babylonia), the north (Media), and the east (Persia).[18] Winged beasts with several heads, lion-eagles, men like animals and such were common in Babylonian imagery. A lion standing on his hind legs as Daniel sees him

(7:4) is often represented in Eastern art. For instance on a seal of King Darius, now in the British Museum, the lion is "set up on feet like a man" before the tree of life. The lion walking in an upright position on the sound box of the lyre from Ur (British Museum) looks as if "the mind of man" (7:4) were given to him. As to the Fourth Beast—Rabbi Simeon (as Rabbi Pinchas and Rabbi Hilkia tell us in his name) as well as ancient Christian commentators wondered why the Fourth Beast is not likened to any known creature.[19] But for the author the Greek kingdom was "different from all kingdoms" (7:23) and he made this idea clear by leaving nameless the monster which not only devoured and crushed the whole world but even "stamped the residue under his feet." *Sh'ar* is the term which the prophets use in promising salvation to the purified "Remnant" of Israel. "The remnant shall return . . . unto the mighty God" (Isa. 10:21). But this remnant was now "stamped" by Epiphanes.

The Fourth Beast has ten horns. Horns symbolized might. A crown of many horns was worn by idols and kings in the Near East. Zechariah (1:18) sees four horns which have scattered Judah, Israel, and Jerusalem. In Daniel's dream another horn, a little one, comes up on the head of the beast. As Porphyry recognized, this is Antiochus IV (Epiphanes), "a contemptible man," who was not in the line of royal succession, but obtained the kingdom "by guile" (Dan. 11:21). Antiochus seized power some weeks after the death of Seleucus IV (on September 3, 175) to protect the rights of the legitimate successor, his nephew, who was a child; but in August 170 he got rid of him.[20]

In the vision, the "little horn" uproots three horns of the beast. According to Porphyry, this refers to Antiochus' victories over Ptolemy VI and VII of Egypt and over Artaxias of Armenia. But the latter was subdued by

Antiochus IV only in 165, at the time when the persecution and the civil war raged in Jerusalem, and the Jews would hardly be concerned about the fate of an Armenian king. In 169, however, Antiochus IV achieved the greatest success of his reign. He triumphed over the three monarchs who since the fall of 170 had jointly reigned in Egypt: Ptolemy VI, Ptolemy VII, and their sister and spouse, Cleopatra II, who, incidentally, was Antiochus' niece. This sensational event directly concerned Jerusalem: returning from his Egyptian campaign, Epiphanes entered the Holy City and plundered the Temple. For the author of the vision of the Four Beasts, the Fourth Empire is no longer a house divided against itself which cannot stand, as Greek domination appeared to the author of Nebuchadnezzar's dream (ch. 2), but the Seleucid empire where ten "horns," ten kings, "arise" in succession (7:24). Antiochus IV was compelled by the Romans to evacuate Egypt in 168. To modern historians, Antiochus' withdrawal of 168 appears as a turning point in history. But to Antiochus' subjects in Jerusalem, who lacked the advantage of hindsight, even after 168 Epiphanes remained the master of the Near East. In 166, he celebrated his triumph in a feast at Antioch and took the title of "Victory-bringing god."

According to the Jewish author, Antiochus IV "arises" as the eleventh horn, and is diverse from the "former kings." The author probably followed the counting of kings which appears in some Babylonian texts: seven Seleucids from Seleucus I to and including Seleucus IV, the predecessor of Antiochus IV, and before them, Alexander the Great, his half brother and successor Philip Arrhidaeus, and Antigonus, who ruled the East before Seleucus I.[21] But, then, the three kings "humbled" by Antiochus IV (7:24) hang in the air, though they correspond to three out of the ten horns (7:8). The author got his symbolism mixed because it was borrowed from Oriental mythology. The number "ten" was for him as conventional as the number "four" in the above mentioned passage of Zechariah. Again, the victory of the fourth king over three others was a motif of Iranian ideology where the number "four" corresponds to the four regions of the world.[22] In fact, neither the author nor the reader was much interested in these details. As Polychronius, a Christian commentator of the fourth century, observes, Daniel does not want to say that Antiochus ruled among ten other kings, but that the Persecutor, who surpassed all kings in evildoing, appeared "when the Macedonian kingdom stood out." Anyway, we cannot expect Aristotelian logic in a dream. As Rabbi Johanan says in the name of Rabbi Simeon ben Johai: just as one cannot have wheat without straw, a prophetic dream always shows some details which are vain.[23]

Daniel now sees God and His court sitting in judgment. The Fourth Beast is condemned and slain and its body burned. The dominion was taken from the other beasts, but their lives were spared. Then came one "in man's likeness," the poetical expression which is mistranslated by the literal rendering "Son of Man." He became invested with the dominion over "all peoples, nations, and languages" for ever. It seems that the author envisages the destruction of the Greek Empire while the Oriental kingdoms shall continue to exist (7:12) "until the [appointed] time and the [due] season." The author here quotes verbatim Daniel 2:21: God "changes times and seasons, removes and sets up kings." He predicts that other Oriental nations also shall become free. This solicitude for the entire Levant is a testimony to Oriental solidarity in the face of the Greeks. In Jewish tradition, Antiochus' spoliations of idolatrous shrines in Persia paralleled his plundering of Jerusalem. The great Jewish rebellion against Rome in 66 C.E. first appeared as the beginning of the general commotion in the East. On the other hand, a Greek historian writing under Augustus could say that the Jews under the Maccabeans were the first of the Orientals to acquire freedom.[24] Yet, since Daniel believes that the greatness of the Hellenic kingdom shall be given in perpetual sovereignty over all the earth to "the holy ones of the Most High" (7:18, 27), he seems to imagine that after the destruction of the Fourth Beast, the world hegemony would be bestowed on the Chosen People.

This interpretation of the vision is given to the dreaming Daniel by an angelic being. As Rabbi Johanan, in agreement with the dream books, says, a dream explained in the midst of a dream is sure to be fulfilled.[25] We learn also from the angel that the Fourth Empire was condemned because of Antiochus' godless arrogance. In the vision the Fourth Beast's mouth was "speaking great things"—the expression was proverbial for boasting. The Psalmist (12:4) speaks of the tongue saying great things: Who is our master? According to First Maccabees (1:24), after robbing the Temple, Antiochus "spoke very presumptuously." The angel explicitly says (7:25) that the Eleventh Horn "uttered words against the Most High." The angel also predicts that the Eleventh Horn will "harass saints of the Most High" and will think of changing "times and law" (7:25). This must refer to some measures of the Reformed Pontiffs, who, backed by Antiochus IV, in 169–67 changed religious calendar and ritual. Ancient religions demanded conformity in cult practices rather than doctrinal unity. The disagreement between the Dead Sea group and the Temple authorities again turned upon the computation of the Day of the Atonement. Esoteric writers attacked the priesthood of Jerusalem for alleged tampering with the calendar. Many centuries later the Karaites refused to recognize the rabbinic calendar. At the end of 167 the whole system of the traditional religion was abolished, the Sabbath and other festivals were prohibited, and the "Abomination of Desolation" was set up on Zion. Thus, our chapter 7 was written between the fall of 169 and the end of 167 B.C.E.

The interpretation does not refer expressly to "the Son of Man." Is he the emblem of the "Saints" to whom the eternal kingdom is promised? Or was this awe-inspiring figure of the far-distant future a subject of esoteric speculations beyond the understanding of the ordinary readers of the tract? The "Saints" or "Saints of the Most High" spoken of in the interpretation of the dream: are they the ideal Israel of the future, or the angelic host, as the terminology of Daniel seems to suggest? The language of revelation is necessarily obscure. Porphyry could identify the "Son of Man" with Judas Maccabaeus; for the Christians the term referred to Christ; for the Jews, to Israel. The author uses traditional imagery and expressions in a new meaning which is ambiguous, since he believes or pretends to believe that he discloses divine secrets. But the esoteric trappings of prophecy only served to enhance the authority of the prediction that the faithful shall be given into the hand of the impious king "for a time, two times, and half a time," that is, as the ancient commentators from Hippolytus to Augustinus recognized, for three and a half years. This was the gist of the revelation. These Jews, remaining faithful to the ancestral religion and customs, hated the Fourth Beast, the blasphemous Greek king and his Jewish henchmen. They were comforted by the prediction that in three years and a half the Enemy would be "consumed and destroyed to the end." Three years and a half is a half of the Sabbatical period. According to the Law the land of Israel had to have a solemn rest every seven years and lie fallow. In

Leviticus (26:34–43) the desolation of the land under foreign domination appears as reparation for the lack of the Sabbatic rest under national rule. The Jews will have to suffer a half of a sabbatic septennium in payment for their disobedience of God's law.

The tract became popular. It seems that when the bloody persecution began in December 167 a new edition of the vision of the Four Beasts was made. The verses 20–22 were added. The "little horn" here becomes greater than its predecessors, and Epiphanes is said to make war against the Saints and to prevail over them.

THE RAM AND THE HE-GOAT (DANIEL 8)

The success of the vision of the Four Beasts led other writers (or perhaps the same writer) to use the same pseudonym and a similar framework for further revelations. It is remarkable that these tracts were composed in the sacred language, probably to enhance their authority. The earliest of them seems to be the vision which now constitutes the eighth chapter of Daniel. The seer is carried in a vision to Susa, the Persian capital. A ram, the zodiacal symbol of Iran, appeared, and no beast could stand before him. But a he-goat, the emblem of Syria, came from the west, and cast down the ram to the ground. Then the seer saw how the great horn of the he-goat was broken and replaced by four horns toward the four winds of heaven, and how a little horn appeared, grew up, and attacked the host of the stars, and even the Prince of the host. The continual burnt offering was taken away from the Prince of the host, the place of his sanctuary destroyed and "the truth was cast down to the ground." We hardly need the interpretation given by the angel

Gabriel: the ram is Persia, the he-goat Greece, the great
horn is Alexander, four horns are the kingdoms of his successors, and the adversary of God is an "insolent king."

The symbolism of the beasts and the device of the
angelic interpreter clearly indicated the dependence of
chapter 8 on chapter 7. But this time Daniel is not dreaming, but experiences his vision when awake and the interpreter is no longer anonymous but is Gabriel himself. As
usual, the imitator tries to overtrump his predecessor.
Some details of the vision are confused since the author
again depended on traditional symbolism. The four kingdoms, according to Porphyry, are Macedonia, Syria, Asia,
and Egypt. But there were no separate kingdoms of Asia
and Syria after Alexander's death. The author speaks of
four kingdoms because he has borrowed the image of the
four winds from chapter 7. As a matter of fact, the sole
reason for the vision is to reveal that Antiochus shall be
broken "by no human hand" and the desolation of the
sanctuary shall end after "two thousand and three hundred evenings and mornings," that is after 1150 days. In
chapter 7, the saints were delivered to Antiochus for "a
year, two years, and half a year." These three and a half
years were already past or were soon to end. The new
vision offered a new promise. As Polychronius noted, the
number of 1150 days corresponds to three years and three
months of a lunar cycle. Thus, Daniel promised the restoration of the Sanctuary to its rightful shape thirty-nine
lunar months after the desecration in Kislev of 167 B.C.E.,
that is, March 163. Such changes of predicted dates, when
the events disagree with the forecast, are common in political prophecies. During the First World War, a prophecy ascribed to St. Odile, the patron of Alsace, promised
the end of German military successes for "the sixth month
of the second year" of the war, that is, for January 1916.
In the spring of 1916, the prophecy was re-edited and now

referred to the Battle of Verdun.[26] The author of chapter 8 of Daniel, who may or may not be the author of chapter 7, needed something more certain than the interpretation of a dream to give courage to his co-religionists during the grim years of the persecution. Gabriel himself now confirmed the fateful date. Yet it again appeared unsatisfactory, and another tract (ch. 9) used a different method of computation.

JEREMIAH REINTERPRETED (DANIEL 9)

In 166 a man in Jerusalem, driven by the stress of the persecution, suddenly apprehended that ancient prophecies, even if already realized according to the common opinion, can bear on the present. Though he made the discovery, as he proudly tells us, by himself (9:2), he confirms it by the authority of Gabriel (9:21).

Jeremiah 25:12 predicted that the desolation of Jerusalem would end after seventy years. For Zechariah (7:5) and the Chronicler (II 36:21) the word had been fulfilled at the restoration of Jerusalem by the Persian king. But this interpretation was no longer satisfactory in 166. The desecration of the Temple in December of 167 and the persecution which followed made evident that the "seventy years" which the nation should serve the king of Babylon (and Antiochus was also the king of Babylon) until God would hearken unto His people (Jer. 29:10) had not been fulfilled as yet. Since God's word cannot be false, it must be re-interpreted, this time with the help of the above described (p. 8) method of *pesher*. "Seventy Years" is a figure for "seventy weeks" of years, that is 490 years. The number 490 always troubled the chronologists, since 490 years, counted from the destruction of the First Temple (587) would bring down the "decreed end" to 97 B.C.E. But Daniel and his readers were not interested in chronology. The point which concerned them was that God's service on Zion would be suspended for "the half of the weeks," that is three and a half years. Counting from the ceasing of the continued burnt offering in the Temple (9:27), that is from about December 15, 167, the seer promised the restoration of Temple worship in the mid-summer of 163. In other words, the author of chapter 9 took over the idea of the sabbatic period of penance from the vision of the Four Beasts (above p. 102), just as he borrowed Gabriel as interpreter from the vision of the ram and the he-goat (above p. 108).

Yet the author tells us that he sought by prayer and supplication, with fasting, sackcloth, and ashes, to obtain the secret of the "Seventy Years" in Jeremiah. For *pesher* is the fruit not of learned interpretation but of inspiration. Ben Sira, elder contemporary of the author of chapter 9, describes how one who knows the Torah seeks out the meaning of prophecies, parables, and proverbs by meditation. Through prayer he would obtain the necessary light. As Gregory the Miracle-Worker, six centuries after Daniel and Ben Sira, so well stated, to understand the prophecies one needs the same divine inspiration which the prophet himself had received.[27]

The method of *pesher* was not new, but the Daniel of chapter 9 applied it to the already realized prophecy. Here he was a revolutionary innovator. It had occurred to no one that the oracle to Croesus (that he would destroy a great kingdom by crossing the river Halys, his frontier with Persia), already realized in his defeat, could have a second meaning realizable generations later. The new insight immediately found favor with clerks of Jerusalem. A new and limitless field opened to their ingenuity. For the author of Daniel 11 (33 ff.) the Suffering Servant of Isaiah (52) is the figure of the steadfast "enlighteners" (*maskilim*) of Epiphanes' persecution. For the author of First Maccabees (7:17) pious Jews slaughtered by a Seleucid general in 161 died "according to the word of the Psalmist" (79:2). The commentator of Habakkuk whose work has been found among the Dead Sea Scrolls was positive that God told the prophets to write down the things that were to come upon the later age. As Paul says (Rom. 15:4): "whatsoever things were written aforetime were written for our learning, that we . . . might have hope." The ancient oracles became perennially valid just as astrological predictions were true indefinitely: the eclipse of the moon in the sign of Taurus means loss of the grain crop.

The passion for *pesher*, which appears so strange to us, was nourished by the classic taste. Ancient authors, writing for civilized readers, liked to display the art of literary allusion. In this way the new sentence became charged with the import of a well-known passage and was illuminated by it. For instance, the words (7:25) that the Enemy shall plan "to change the times and the seasons" evoked for the author and his hearers the words of Daniel to Nebuchadnezzar (2:21) that God "changes the times and the seasons"; Antiochus dared to equal the Almighty. But the allusion also reminded the reader of Daniel's warning addressed to Nebuchadnezzar in the same breath, that God removes and installs kings at His pleasure. In Isaiah 14:13 the King of Babylon thinks to exalt his throne above the stars of God. Speaking of the arrogance of Antiochus, who was also the king of Babylon, Daniel (8:10) and later the author of Second Maccabees refer to Isaiah's words. Daniel's book, like Ecclesiastes written some twenty years before, is full of reminiscences of Jewish classics.

But when a prophecy in this manner refers to an earlier prophecy, it is easy for the author and his readers to imagine that the ancient oracle has been or would be realized now. How could Daniel doubt that the word of Balaam (Num. 24:24) speaking of the ships of Kittim which shall afflict Asshur, a prophecy that seems to have no sense for the time of Balaam, a contemporary of Moses, was fulfilled when the "Kittim" of his own days, the Romans, in 168 expelled Antiochus, who was also the lord of Assyrian country, from Egypt (11:3)? Again, Jeremiah's words (30:7) that now is the time of Jacob's trouble, "yet he shall be saved out of it," sounded to the ear of Daniel (12:1) like the prediction of Epiphanes' persecution.

Moses warns (Deut. 28:50) that to punish the apostasy, the Lord will bring a nation of "fierce countenance" that shall have no regard for the old nor for the young. Daniel sees this prophecy fulfilled in his own time when the persecution immediately followed apostasy. He calls Epiphanes a king "of fierce countenance." *On n'entend les prophéties que quand on voit les choses arrivées* (Pascal).

HISTORY REVISITED
(DANIEL 10–12)

The last tract published under the name of Daniel (ch. 10–12) is the strangest of all. It is neither a dream (ch. 7), nor a vision (ch. 8). Like the interpretation of the Seventy Years (9:23) it is a "word" (10:1) delivered by an angel to a wakeful Daniel. But here the "word" is the account of "the entries in the register of truth" (10:21), that is, of the heavenly book of destinies (7:10; 12:1). In Greece, the Fates spun the web of destiny. In the Near East, the bureaucratic gods fixed the future by making entries on clay tablets or in papyrus rolls. When Ezekiel (3:1) is commissioned as a prophet, he eats a heavenly scroll which contains "lamentations and mourning and woe" to befall his generation. The angel makes Daniel know "what shall befall thy people in the latter days" (10:14). As in the vision of the ram and the he-goat (8:17, 26), the revelation is to be kept concealed until the appointed time. But now it is not the verbal message but a book which remains sealed (12:4). The imitator again overtrumps the model.

The angel announces the course of history from Cyrus to Epiphanes. It is prefigured, and thus predetermined, by the fights between the celestial princes of Persia and Greece and the angel Gabriel, who is aided by Michael, the heavenly patron of the Chosen People (10:13, 20). The future events are indicated allusively: "The daughter of the king of the South shall come to the King of the North, to establish an agreement . . ." (11:6). As Ibn Ezra says: "The Angel dictated and Daniel wrote in enigmas." In fact, Daniel here imitates the style of contemporary astrologers who announced, for instance, that the daggerlike comet in the north portends "the mixing of northern and Libyan peoples: a daughter of the Libyan ruler would be given in marriage to the Lord of the North, and she would plot against the father and betray him because of her impious love for the husband." [28]

It is natural that the far-distant Persian period should be dealt with briefly. Four kings will follow Cyrus. As Porphyry saw, Daniel means Smerdis, Cambyses, Darius I, and his son Xerxes, "who will stir up all against the realm of Greece" (11:2). (Daniel here uses Isaiah 38:17, which speaks of the Medes.) The nine kings who ruled Persia after Xerxes are passed over in silence, and the seer now mentions Alexander, "the mighty king," who in this way, in agreement with the official Macedonian version, appears as the avenger of Hellas wronged by Xerxes.

After Alexander and the division of his empire (11:4), the history is confined to wars and pacts between the Seleucids and the Ptolemies of Egypt. Poised on the frontier between these two great realms, Jerusalem was deeply involved in the rapports between the kings of the North and the kings of the South (Egypt). The pro-Syrian and the pro-Egyptian factions fought for the soul of Jerusalem. The modern reader cannot but be amazed at the amount of knowledge of contemporary history which Daniel expects from his hearers, such as the marriage of Antiochus II and Berenice of Egypt, celebrated ninety years before (252), in the mention of the daughter of the King of the South.

This survey of history is even more detailed for the reign and the actions of Epiphanes. The author describes the pollution of the Temple and the persecution, and even knows that in the midst of adversity the Jews will receive "a little help" (11:34), a reference (as Porphyry recognized) to the first successes of the Maccabees. The tract, accordingly, was composed not before the summer of 166. But at this point the foreknowledge of the angel ends, and from now on Daniel announces things that never happened. He does not know Antiochus' eastern campaign, which began in the spring of 165. He looks southward and predicts that the time of the end is coming and would be opened by a revanche offensive of Egypt (11:40). But Antiochus will come against Egypt "like a whirlwind" and will triumph over his enemies. Antiochus will plant his "palace-tents" (that is the royal tent of the military camp) west of Jerusalem—"between the sea and the holy mountain"—and he "shall come to his end, and none shall help him" (11:45). Daniel does not say how the Persecutor would perish. He probably has in mind the promises of 2:34 and 8:25 that the Enemy will "be broken without human hand," that is, through a direct intervention of God. Yet it is remarkable that, having seen and exactly described (11:30) the Roman intervention of 168, two years later Daniel does not realize that Rome would not tolerate the conquest of Egypt, Libya and Ethiopia (11:43) by the Seleucids. Daniel is not interested, however, in the balance of power, but looks forward to the Last Judgment. "At that time," after the Persecutor's end, Michael, the celestial prince of Israel, shall stand up for the children of the Chosen People. A time of the last affliction comes, but all pious souls, "all who are found registered in the Book," shall be saved (12:1).

THE PROPHET LOOKING BACKWARD (DANIEL 10–12)

The soothsayer, who like a historian looks backward and describes the past as if it were the future before uttering the real predictions, is a strange figure in the line of biblical prophets, and in Oriental divination generally. There are collections of Akkadian predictions[29] which announce, for instance, that a prince will rule for thirteen years, that in his reign the Elamites will attack and destroy the shrines of the great gods of Akkad, and so on. Copied one after another, so that "good" and "bad" reigns mostly alternate, these prophecies, just like the above quoted prognostications (p. 114), remain disjointed, and offer no survey of history down to the time of the editor.

An Egyptian text (the so-called "Demotic Chronicle"), written in the middle of the fourth century, feigns to have been composed before the reign of Nectanebus II (359–342). Its author uses the method of *pesher*. For instance, an obscure text enumerated seven days of a month, the seventh being consecrated to the god Ptah. The interpretation refers the first six days to the six pharaohs who preceded Nectanebus II, and who here are mentioned by their names, while the day of Ptah indicates the future king (Nectanebus II) who remains unnamed.

In fact, the vaticination style of Daniel 10–12 was Greek, and for this reason Porphyry easily recognized the trick. From Aeschylus' *Persians* (472) on, Greek poets, following the example of the Greek seers, freely used the device of re-telling history as if it were the future. In Aristophanes' parody, Bakis, a famous seer of old, predicts that Athens will be ruled by an oakum-seller (the demagogue Eucrates), then by a sheep-seller (Lysicles), then a leather-seller, that is, Cleon, who was at the height of his power in 424 when Aristophanes produced *The Knights*. But the oracle also promises that Cleon will be overtrumped by a sausage-seller, an even more impudent fellow. Needless to say, this genuine "prediction" was never realized.

Two examples may suffice to illustrate the vogue of this prognostic device in political propaganda at the time of Daniel. About 187 a prophecy circulated in Greece, allegedly uttered by a vaticinating Roman consul in 191. The prophecy exactly described the military events which happened in 191–188. But the Consul's trance then sees Italy invaded and enslaved by the King of Asia (that is Antiochus III). In fact, the Seleucid, defeated in 189, never tried to exact from Rome his revenge. When in 197 the advance of the Roman army was temporarily checked in Macedonia, a Sibylline oracle announced to the Greeks that after the defeat of the Punics by the Trojan race, that is, the Romans (in 203), and the apparition of a new island (this volcanic event happened in 198) "worse men" shall prevail over "the better ones." In June of the same year, 197, the Roman victory at Cynoscephale realized this adroit prophecy. Three hundred years later Plutarch still quoted it as the indubitable proof of man's capacity to know the future.

Even the form of Daniel's inverted prophecy is Greek. In the poem of Lycophron, Cassandra vaticinates at the time when Paris is sailing to Troy with Helena. The prophetess predicts the Trojan war, and the subsequent struggles between Asia and Europe. After having surveyed a millennium, she promises the pact between the descendants of the Trojans (the Romans) and the successors of Alexander, which would end the conflict between the two continents for ever. Alas, on this point Cassandra and Lycophron, her speaker, were mistaken.

The popularity of the device used by Lycophron and Daniel is easily understandable. To quote Philo again: "The fulfillment in the past is the guaranty of the realization in the future." [30] The fulfillment of a series of predictions in their chronological order was even more impressive. The sceptics could say that an isolated prediction tossed forth into the infinity of time "as if it were into the sea," may be fulfilled by mere chance. But (to quote Plutarch) what about the oracles that state not only what shall come to pass, but how and when and after what and attended by what? The argument seemed unanswerable, and the inverted series of predictions enjoyed favor for about 2500 years. We read for instance in Livy that in 213 two prophecies of the seer Marcius became known. The first one predicted the Roman disaster at Cannae (216) and, its "authority" being confirmed by the outcome, it "lent credibility" to the other, the time of which had not yet come: the seer commanded the Romans to establish a festival to Apollo if

they wished to drive out the enemy. The festival was
founded in 212, and, verily, Hannibal had to abandon
Italy ten years later. Merlin, his rivals and imitators in
the Middle Ages and afterwards, and political prophecies
in both world wars exhibit the same pattern.

THE PSEUDONYMOUS PROPHECY

We have seen why the apocalyptics in 168–66 chose
the pseudonym of Daniel. But why did they need a
pseudonym? From Amos to Malachi the prophets of
Israel spoke in their own names to their contemporaries.
On the other hand, a prediction naturally concerns the
present. One asks the oracle or a gypsy whether one's
plan will succeed, but not about the yet unborn generation. Why cause a man who lived four centuries before
to prophesy about Antiochus Epiphanes? Our textbooks
tell us that for the Jews of the Hellenistic Age the
canonized Torah left no room for prophecy, so that inspiration was a thing of the past. This simplicist explanation does not make Daniel more intelligible.

In fact, seers were not lacking in Persian and Hellenistic Jerusalem. Prophets and prophetesses opposed
Nehemiah in 444 (Neh. 6:14), and the enemies asserted
that he appointed prophets himself to proclaim him king
(Neh. 6:7). In 200, during the war between Antiochus
IV and Ptolemy V, some men rose "to establish the
vision" (Dan. 11:14). A century later, Judas, one of the
Essenes, was known for the veracity of his predictions
and, as Josephus tells us, had companions and friends who
dwelt with him in order to learn how to foretell the
future. The Gospels and Josephus attest that in the last
decades of the Second Temple the prophetic spirit was
overflowing Judah and Jerusalem. Josephus himself had

the revelation that Vespasian would become Emperor.

Yet these seers did not inspire confidence. In 164 the stones of the polluted altar were put aside until the coming of a prophet to say what should be done with them (I Macc. 9:27). This means: until the prophet appears who, as Ben Sira prays (36:15) shall indubitably speak in the name of God. Josephus stated that after Artaxerxes Jewish history was less trustworthy "because there was no longer an exact succession of the prophets." In other words, as Jesus experienced (Matt. 13:57), a prophet is not without honor, save in his own country and in his own house. Why?

The Greeks, following the Babylonians, distinguished between natural and artificial divination. The latter was a scientific technique of inference: if the Sun rises when Mars is in Gemini, some men will rebel against the king in the country of Syria.[31] On the other hand, revelation in vision and dream was a divine gift vouchsafed to the elect: be it Amos or a man who in the eighteenth century B.C.E. heard in a dream from the god Dagon the promise of victory for the king of Mari. In the middle of the sixth century B.C.E. when the future tyrant Peisistratus marched on Athens, a frenzied seer, on the spur of the moment, predicted his success. Such examples make it clear why the ecstatic prophecy was repressed or tamed in democratic Athens as well as in the Persian monarchy and the Jerusalem of the High Priests.

Simon Maccabaeus in 141 insisted that there was now no trustworthy prophet. The hierarchy wanted to monopolize the gift of inspiration. This is the meaning of the doctrine expressed in the Fourth Gospel (11:51) that the High Priest knows the future. This doctrine is illustrated by the anecdotes transmitted by Josephus and the rabbis about the predictions made by the High Priests

Simeon the Just and John Hyrcanus. In Greece the
Pythia was a survival of ecstatic prophecy, and her in-
coherent words were interpreted by the Delphic clergy.
For Aeschylus, Cassandra is possessed by her god and
foretells in frenzy but is not believed by anybody. About
a half-century before the Athenian dramatist, a Jewish
seer (Zech. 13:3) had announced the coming of the age
when the ecstatic prophet would be brought to shame
through his vision. As Cicero, a Roman consul, succinctly
put it: if gods wished to communicate with the Roman
people, why should they do it through the medium of
some unknown man and not address a leader of the
State? [32] Divine madness was now, as Plato says,[33] license
of poets and illusion of lovers.

Yet no divinatory technique can substitute for the
inspired utterance of a seer when the spirit of his god
comes upon him. When man asks questions or interprets
signs, his ignorance obstructs the divine message. The cry
of a seated eagle on the right has no meaning for the man
except as he relates it to his own doings. Pythia could
pry into the distant future (once she predicted the succession of eight kings at Cyrene), but generally she had
to speak of matters which were of immediate import to
the inquirer. A simple man asked the seer where to find
the lost asses (I Sam. 9:6). A king inquired: "Shall I go
against Ramoth-Gilead to battle, or should I forbear?"
(I Kings 22:6).

The sole "natural" divination, necessarily tolerated
by the State, was imparted in dreams, but dreams were
deceptive. Only the direct revelation was both true and
far reaching. As Heraclitus says, with raving lips the
Sibyl uttered a voice which reached over a thousand
years. Accordingly, makers of propaganda turned to the
books of ancient seers whose authority was indubitable.
As early as c. 520 a Greek oracle-monger by the name

of Onomocritus was caught interpolating words into the prophecies of Musaeus, a venerable author supposed to have lived several centuries before. From Athens, Onomocritus went to Persia and again fabricated oracles of Musaeus, which served to induce Xerxes to make war on Athens. A political vaticination of a potter on the future of Egypt, allegedly spoken before the ancient pharaoh Amenophis, circulated in Persian, Greek, and Roman Egypt. Collections of prophecies of the Sibyls, of Bakis and Musaeus, continued to circulate in the Greek world through centuries.

The Sibyl who had already predicted the Trojan war was also a good authority to anticipate the result of the battle of Chaeronea (338), the outcome of Epiphanes' campaigns, and even to announce the last age of mankind in Vergil's Fourth Eclogue. The Jews and then the Christians also circulated oracles under her name, and she continued to prophesy in the Middle Ages. In the days of Daniel the predictions of the Sibyls, of Enoch and Zoroaster and so on, were easily to be found at the nearest bookstore. These oracles were obscure, and for this reason inspired confidence. God, as Heraclitus says of Apollo of Delphi, "neither speaks out, nor conceals, but gives a sign." [34] The authors of these oracles lived in the long-distant past and for this reason were credible. A seer of today could easily be hired by a politician, but how can Musaeus or Zoroaster be bribed today? The words of these ancient seers could be interpreted variously. In the Sibylline oracles there was no precise indication of the persons spoken of nor of the time of fulfillment. This imprecision confirmed the authenticity of the predictions. Zeus wished prophetic utterances to be incomplete so that men, afraid of the future, would continue to care for the gods.[35]

THE FULFILLED PROPHECY

In Greece the glory of the oracles was tarnished by the failure of many predictions. In Hellenistic Jerusalem nobody doubted the word of Isaiah or Jeremiah. The four scrolls of the great prophets and a volume of the sayings of the twelve minor prophets had been collected long ago, according to the tradition, by Nehemiah. Thus, nobody would be able to circulate a new oracle attributed to one of the recognized messengers of God. Besides, the latter obviously spoke to their contemporaries except in some predictions which announced the Day of the Lord in an indefinite future. As Ben Sira shows, around 200 B.C.E. the classical prophets were taken as witnesses to past events, to the sins of Israel of old and to the inexhaustible mercy of the Deity and love for the Chosen People. The ancient prophecies contained warnings and promises of permanent import, but no prediction concerning the course of events in Seleucid Jerusalem.

But in the Jerusalem of Antiochus Epiphanes men needed more than ever understanding of the divine plan and reassurance about the future. Happily, there circulated stories about a wise man of old, who "had understanding of all visions and dreams" (Dan. 1:17) and whose actions and revelations bore directly on the troubles of the present. In the teeth of foreign oppressors, face to face with Nebuchadnezzar, Belshazzar and Darius, he preserved the ancestral faith, was delivered from the den of lions, and, above all, in the days of Nebuchadnezzar announced the coming of the Grecian kingdom, and promised that it would be overthrown by the God of Heavens, and be followed by the establishment of the reign of God.

When we read the revelations of Daniel now, we must realize that to their first hearers during the years of persecution the whole apparatus of the visions, beasts, angels and Daniel's swoons (8:18) was of secondary importance. What they asked was: "Watchman, what of the night?" (Isa. 21:11). The oracles of Daniel answered that the night of persecution would continue for a half of the Sabbatical period, that is for three and a half years (7:25; 9:27; 12:7). But when the predicted time approached and no deliverance was yet in sight, more prudent and more exact calculations were made: two thousand and three hundred evenings and mornings, that is, 1150 days "until the Sanctuary be cleansed" (8:14). The abomination would continue for 1290 days, says an addition to the last tract (12:11). "Blessed is he who waits and comes to 1135 days," corrected a second interpolator (12:12).

They all were wrong, they all were of too little faith. The Persecution ended in March 164, the Temple was recovered (approximately) in November, and the legitimate cult restored on Kislev 25, that is about December 15 of the same year, about 1100 days, less than three and a half years after the Abomination of Desolation had been placed on the Altar. Some weeks later the news arrived that the Persecutor had suddenly died, stricken by some mysterious disease. As Daniel promised (8:25; 11:45), Antiochus, at the height of his might, was broken "without hand" (8:25) and there was "none to help him" (11:45).

What mattered now that Daniel was mistaken in some details, for instance, that the Enemy ended not in the Holy Land (11:45) but in far-away Isfahan? Daniel also predicted the establishment of the divine reign after the end of the Oppressor. But he also said (12:1) that it would be preceded by a time of affliction "such as never

was," and Jerusalem had had enough woes in the last
five years to be sorry that the kingdom of God was not
at hand.

The prophets of old, the prophets whose oracles
were studied by the sages, spoke generally of punishment
for apostasy and promised the restoration of the Chosen
People. Daniel predicted almost the exact date of the
salvation. For the first (and last) time in the history of
the Chosen People a long-range prophecy, uttered more
than three hundred fifty years before, was fulfilled literally and in all details that mattered.

To the generations that followed, who no longer
cared about the horrors of Epiphanes' persecution, Daniel
was the prophet who made sense of history. It is not
accidental that the Church appropriated his calculation
of the Seventy Weeks and that his scheme of Four Monarchies dominated historical thinking until Jean Bodin
(1530–96).

For the Greeks, the fathers of our historical method,
history had no finality. Lycophron surveys history from
Herakles to the Roman domination, but the final rec-
onciliation between the West and the East which he
predicts at the end makes the millennium of the pre-
ceding wars even more senseless. Neither the eternity of
Roman domination, promised in Vergil's *Aeneid*, nor
the Savior from Herakleopolis, announced in the "Demotic Chronicle," makes sense in the frame of universal
history. The promise of the Sibyl which opens Vergil's
Fourth Eclogue is even more saddening: the cyclic return of the Golden Age will be inexorably followed by
a new degradation and fall.

For Daniel, history reveals the purpose of the Creator. His visions seem to be dominated by blind determinism. Kingdoms and kings succeed by a kind of fatality. Why should the ram and the he-goat fight? Why

are the beasts dissimilar? Daniel does not inquire about this of the interpreting angels. He knows that the nations punish Israel for her sins. "We have sinned . . . all Israel has transgressed Thy Law . . . as it is written in the Law of Moses . . . all this evil has come upon us . . ." (ch. 9). When the evildoings of the Gentiles reach the culmination, as in the persecution of Epiphanes, God will intervene and save His people. As we have noted, though a witness of the Roman intervention in Egypt, Daniel does not think that Rome or any other human force (including the Maccabees) will overthrow the Tyrant. In this case the Fifth Monarchy (as really happened) would succeed the Macedonian rule and thus deprive the sufferings of the martyrs and the whole course of history of any meaning. But history must be meaningful, and in the world created by the Creator out of nothing, the finality of history must be the kingdom of God.

Knowing that God is just, Daniel under Belshazzar and Cyrus could foresee the march and direction of history, which for him was not the accidental sequence of events, but led to redemption and the reign of justice. How beautiful, says Pascal, is it to see with the eyes of faith Cyrus, Alexander, the Ptolemies and the Seleucids all unwittingly acting for the glory of God. Firm in his faith, Daniel remembered the meaning of the years to come. *E degli anni ancor non nati Daniel si ricorda* (A. Manzoni).

Porphyry and His Successors

PORPHYRY

The Book of Daniel narrates deeds and reproduces predictions of the prophet Daniel who allegedly lived in the second half of the sixth century B.C.E. In fact, it was compiled in 166 B.C.E. to comfort and encourage the Jews of Judea and Jerusalem persecuted by Antiochus Epiphanes. It is the only book of the Bible of which the origin and purpose can be known with certainty.

This discovery was not made in the ivory tower of objective scholarship. Biblical criticism was not born as an antiquarian pastime or in the pursuit of naked truth. It was—and still is for some people—a war engine hurling missiles against the citadel of faith. For the Christians, the incontrovertible proof of their faith was the fulfillment of the "Old Testament" prophecies in Jesus. Let pagans pretend that Jesus had established his worship by magic arts. Augustine[36] maintains that by no magic could Jesus make the prophets who had preceded him predict his coming, deeds and death. A collection of biblical testimonies referring to Jesus was one of the first works of Christian propaganda. Of course, the Christians did not invent this kind of demonstration. The sectaries of the Dead Sea, for instance, also believed that the Bible was full of predictions concerning them and their "Teacher of Righteousness." But this group disappeared in the catastrophe of 70 C.E., while the authority of the

Church supported the Christian interpretation of Hebrew oracles. No lesser man than Blaise Pascal (1623–62) could state that "the greatest proof of Jesus Christ is the prophecy."

Of all messianic prophecies, the most important was the testimony of Daniel. Daniel, as Josephus says, "not only prophesied of future events, but also determined the time of their fulfilment." In the Gospels, Jesus applies to himself the words of Daniel that the Son of a Man shall come in the clouds of heaven. Daniel, says Augustine in the *City of God*,[37] even defined the exact date of the coming and suffering of Christ. Jerome said that none of the prophets spoke so clearly concerning Christ: Daniel sets forth the very time at which Jesus would come and announces beforehand the clearest signs of events to come. Thirteen centuries later, Isaac Newton stated that to disbelieve Daniel's predictions "is to reject the Christian religion. For this religion is founded upon his prophecy concerning the Messiah."

It was a pagan enemy of the new faith who deliberately set out to overthrow the prophetic proof of Christianity. The Neo-Platonic philosopher Porphyry, c. 260, published a treatise *Against the Christians* in fifteen books, of which the twelfth established the thesis that the Book of Daniel was not composed by the ancient prophet of this name, but by someone living in the time of Antiochus Epiphanes and making his oracles in order to revive the hopes of his countrymen during persecution. Porphyry's main point was that the author agrees with history so long as he speaks of events until the time of Antiochus, and is in error beyond this point. He did not foreknow the future, but alluded to past events.

The "sacrilegious curiosity" of Porphyry, to use Augustine's words,[38] is almost lost to us. The copies of his work were destroyed by Christian Emperors and the refutations written by Christian apologists were forgotten, so that today we know only some fragments, reproduced at second hand, by Jerome in his commentary on Daniel and by some other Christian compilers. Jerome implicitly acknowledges the validity of Porphyry's method, saying that the predictions of Daniel were fulfilled with such precision that to the infidels the prophet seems not to be foretelling the future but reporting the past. Yet Jerome and other Christian sources never mention the essential argument of Porphyry: the false predictions of Daniel. According to Jerome, even the resurrection of the dead was understood by Daniel (12:2) as a metaphor describing the salvation of the Jews after the death of Antiochus IV. But if Daniel's prophecies referred only to past events, how could his oracles encourage his brethren? Jerome, who neglects to reproduce Porphyry's interpretation of the Seventy Weeks, the main article of christological computation, probably also suppressed the passages where Porphyry demonstrated the inauthenticity of Daniel. Jerome did not write to preserve Porphyry's memory, but to help his pious friends, Pammachus and Marcella, carry on war against the blasphemous adversaries of Christ. We can still recognize a passage which to Porphyry must have appeared as a false prophecy. According to Daniel 2:40, the Fourth Empire was to be crushed by a big stone. The Jews "and the impious Porphyry" understood the stone as a symbol of Israel which would crush all realms and rule forever. Porphyry rightly identified the Fourth Beast (and thus the Fourth Empire) as referring to the Macedonian monarchy. He must have regarded the prophecy that after Antiochus IV the Jews would dominate the world and "stand forever" as patently misleading and concocted by Pseudo-Daniel to inspire his people with confidence. For Jerome and the Jews of his time, however, the Fourth Empire meant Rome.

Porphyry did not invent a new method. Literary forgeries abounded in Greek and Roman literature, and religious books, pagan, Jewish, and Christian, were often put into circulation under the name of some ancient worthy. As soon as the Jews learned enough Greek, they began to fabricate the texts of famous Greek authors which glorified the Chosen People. As early as 150, Christians concocted the minutes of Jesus' trial. During the great persecution in 311, Roman authorities manufactured false acts of the same trial. A century later Augustine knew the apocryphal letters of Jesus, in which he appeared as a magician.

Greek scholars usually detected an apocryphal work by using the criterion of anachronisms. For instance Dionysius of Halicarnassus proves that a speech attributed to the Athenian orator Deinarchus cannot be authentic. For this speech refers to some event of the year 352 B.C.E., according to our reckoning. But at this date Deinarchus was only ten years old. Eusebius in his *Church History*[39] denies the authenticity of pagan acts of Jesus' trial by the same method: in these acts the date of the trial corresponds to the seventh year of Tiberius, but Pilate did not become governor of Judea before the twelfth year of this emperor. Long before Dionysius and Eusebius, a critic of Plato by the name of Herodicus impugned the credibility of Socratic dialogues by enumerating anachronisms committed by Plato and Xenophon.

Porphyry, author of a great work on chronology which covered the period from the Trojan war (1184 B.C.E.) to his own times (268 C.E.) was particularly qualified for such demolition work. He had also proved that a book bearing the name of Zoroaster was "a counter-

feited new book," published to support some new ideas
with the authority of the Persian prophet. Its authors
"having deceived themselves also deceived many others."
He regarded the story of Jesus walking on the sea of
Galilee as an invention. But he rejected the story not
because it was miraculous but for chronological reasons.
The disciples sailed "when evening came" and Jesus
walked on water to rescue them "about the fourth watch
of the night" (Mark 6:45), that is some ten hours later.
Yet this lake can be crossed by the simplest boat in two
hours. Porphyry was also a brilliant philologist who could
end a fruitless discussion by showing that the perplexing
reading in Plato was erroneous.[40] However, he did not
know Hebrew (Aramaic). He studied Daniel in a very
imperfect Greek version which became part of the Greek
Bible used in the Church. Thus his guesses, brilliant as
they were, were often mistaken. But his chronological
thesis, that the Book of Daniel was written during the
persecution of Antiochus Epiphanes (between 169 and
165, as we now can establish) has stood the test of time.

AFTER PORPHYRY

Thanks to Jerome's Commentary on Daniel, the
ideas of Porphyry became known to the Christian Occi-
dent, but his refutation of Porphyry's "fallacy" appeared
so successful to his pious readers that the words of the
impious "deceiver" did not endanger the christological
interpretation of the prophetic book.

It seems that a Jewish miscreant who did not know
anything about Porphyry's objections was the first modern author to impugn the authenticity of the Book of
Daniel. Uriel d'Acosta (1647) refused to accept it on
account of the belief in resurrection intimated in Daniel

12. He also adduced the names of angels in the book, and its style generally. For him Daniel was "a clever invention" of the Pharisees (who believed in immortality and angels), that is, of the sect which, he asserted, had corrupted the genuine Law of Moses. It is curious that Spinoza, also ignorant of Porphyry but acquainted with the work of d'Acosta, could assert that chapters 8–12 of Daniel, written in Hebrew and in the first person, were undoubtedly from the pen of the ancient prophet. Hobbes, who must have known Jerome's commentary and thus Porphyry's view, prudently abstained from comment on this perilous subject. Newton could ascribe the compilation of the Pentateuch to Samuel and was ready to believe that the stories about Daniel (ch. 1–6) were not written by the prophet himself, but the authenticity of christological prophecies was for him an article of faith.

The rationalist John Marsham seems to have been the first Christian scholar who dared state that Daniel's computation of Seventy Weeks refers not to the coming of Christ but to Antiochus Epiphanes (in his *Chronicus Canon*, 1672, a very technical work on time-reckoning). His contemporary Henry Dodwell (1641–1711), who was bold enough to write that the number of Christian martyrs was very small, agreed with Marsham in the interpretation of the Seventy Weeks, but his opinion was made public by his biographer only after his death.[41]

It was the English deist Anthony Collins who, probably led by Dodwell's remark, in 1727 "followed the steps of Porphyry," as the pious Thomas Newton regretfully stated in his *Dissertation on the Prophets* (1754). Collins, in his *Scheme of Literary Prophecy Considered*, answered Bishop Chandler's *Defense of Christianity from the Prophecies of the Old Testament*. Following Porphyry, he offered the proof that the Book of

Daniel had been written by a counterfeit author and that the prophecies of Daniel, understood literally, referred to Antiochus Epiphanes. His book scandalized English divines and provoked numerous refutations. Yet the influence of his work was hardly noticeable at first. It was never reprinted, yet the words of the pious refutation cited above are taken from Thomas Newton's eighth edition, printed in 1787.

Collins, a friend of Locke, believed that free-thinking was the cure for atheism. The more decided adversaries of established religion did not care much for historical criticism, but directed their attacks against the philosophical and moral aspects of Scripture. The reason was that for Christians as for Jews the Scriptures are not a venerable document of sacred history but God's word. Neither human authors nor their relation to the history of their own time can matter. Commenting on Job in 585 Gregory the Great refuses to discuss the superfluous question of authorship since the real writer of the book was the Holy Ghost. Receiving a letter, we do not inquire by which pen it was written. In turn, Voltaire ("Examen du Milord Bolingbroke") exclaims that to inquire about the author of the Pentateuch is foolish. "I consider as the most futile of all researches to try to find out the name of the author of the ridiculous book." As in a fun house mirror, the thought of Voltaire reflects the idea of Gregory the Great.

When at the end of his life Voltaire summarized the work of the rationalists (*La Bible enfin expliquée*), he stated casually that the critics asserted that Daniel was written in the time of Antiochus Epiphanes. Neither here nor elsewhere does he refer to Porphyry's argument. He was bored by the apocalyptical book, which he calls a "roman," and was more interested in making jokes about Nebuchadnezzar transformed into a bull ("La Princesse de Babylon"). Although Voltaire repeatedly (as in the *Essai sur les moeurs*, ch. 9) insinuated that canonic gospels may be forgeries like the apocryphal stories of Jesus, he obviously did not realize the methodological value of Porphyry's discovery.

The same is true for other free-thinkers. The atheist S. Maréchal in his *Pour et Contre la Bible* (1801), speaking of Daniel, is satisfied with flat jokes. Thomas Paine in *The Age of Reason* (1795), says that there is no inherent evidence to prove that Daniel and Ezekiel were not written by their supposed authors. He defends the authenticity of these books, however full of unintelligible visions. Their authors wrote in this style "because it was unsafe" in the Exile "to speak facts or plain language."

Biblical scholarship in the eighteenth century became virtually a monopoly of German Protestant theologians. They paid no attention to the dilettante Collins. The standard *Introduction to the Old Testament* by J. G. Carpzow, in the edition of 1757, states that Porphyry's objections have been rebutted by Jerome. Likewise, the manual of the next theological generation, the *Einleitung* of J. G. Eichhorn, in the edition of 1790, neglects to answer Porphyry. The author, however, stresses many improbable details in the stories about Daniel and suggests that only the prophetic visions are authentic. Eichhorn is quite proud of this discovery and omits mentioning that his hypothesis had already been formulated in France and England almost a century before. In the next edition (1803),[42] Eichhorn inserted a new paragraph, pedantically numbered 615b, where he suddenly followed Porphyry and assigned Daniel's visions to the time of Antiochus Epiphanes. A discreet note refers to two anonymous books published in 1781 and 1783.

It is characteristic of academic scholarship that the

latter two works, written by Heinrich Corrodi (1752–93), could sway scholarly opinion.[43] Corrodi was an extremist of the *Aufklärung* who opposed the "rational religion" to "fanaticism." He simply repeats the objections of Porphyry and the arguments of Marchant, and prudently refrains from endorsing Porphyry's contention that the author of Daniel was a forger. What he adds is an academic qualification (he was a disciple of J. S. Semler, a leading theologian of his age) and the spirit of Lutheran intolerance. Jesus' religion was rational. Therefore, everything in the New Testament that disagrees with the *Vernunft* is judaizing. Corrodi heaps scorn and abuse on the rabbis and their Talmud, prudently adding that in the older times of the Old Testament revelation the Jewish religion was not so bad. The anti-Christianity of Collins did not hurt; the anti-Judaism of Corrodi helped to glorify the "rational" faith of German professors and to forward "rational" thinking in the matters of religion. Religion had to serve the moral purpose and Corrodi, disagreeing with Luther, particularly praised the Letter of James. Besides, his view was presented in a scholarly dignified manner, in the first part of the first volume of a *Critical History*. Accepted in the authoritative handbook of Eichhorn and in the influential commentary of L. Bertholdt (1806), the thesis of Porphyry at last won the field because it was a weapon in the hand of rationalism and then of so-called liberal Protestantism.

NOTES TO DANIEL

1. I owe this explanation of the pseudonym "Daniel" to my colleague G. Cohen.

2. See the papers of S. A. Kaehler and H. Reinicke in the *Nachrichten* of the Academy of Göttingen, 1954 and 1955.

3. *Bereshit Rabba* 52.5.

4. Macrobius *Somnium Scipionis* 3.2; *Berakoth* 55a. In difficult cases Assyrian kings asked several classes of diviners for advice. Cf. H. Talmon, *Eretz-Israel* V (1958), pp. 150 ff. This was done, probably, to check the veracity of the answer. Daniel uses the motif as a device for contrasting the ignorance of the pagan sages with his hero's sagacity.

5. T. Zielinski, *Iresione* (1931), pp. 425 ff.

6. H. Lewy, *Studies in Honor of S. H. Taqizadeh* (1962), p. 140.

7. H. L. Ginsberg, *Studies in Daniel* (1948), p. 26.

8. S. Lieberman, *Hellenism in Jewish Palestine* (1950), p. 70.

9. E. Cassin, *Revue de l'histoire des religions*, CXXXIX (1951), p. 129. Cf. G. Furlani, "La sentenza del Dio," in *Memorie dell' Accademia dei Lincei*, Series 21, VIII (1950). When Zoroaster comes to King Vishtaspa, the wise men of the court plot against him and he is put into prison on faked evidence, but wins the king by a miracle (A. V. W. Jackson, *Zoroaster* [1898], p. 61).

10. O. Eissfeldt, *Zeitschrift für die alttestamentliche Wissenschaft*, LXXII (1960), p. 134.

11. *Wayikra Rabba* 33.6.

12. M. Molé, *Le problème zoroastrien* (1963), p. 33: God Ahuramazda told Zoroaster that neither fire nor molten metal nor sword would compel his followers to disavow the "true religion." Cf. S. H. Taqizadeh, *Bulletin of the School of Oriental and African Studies*, VIII (1935–37), p. 392. King Peroz (459–84) proved his innocence by a fire ordeal: the flames of the sacred fire reached his beard, but did not hurt him. See al-Buruni, Chronology, tr. E. Sachau (1879), p. 215.

13. J. Milik, *Revue Biblique*, LXIII (1956), p. 411.

14. *Syria*, XXV (1946–48), p. 67.

15. J. and L. Robert, "Bulletin épigraphique," No. 121, in *Revue des études grecques*, LXIX (1956).

16. O. R. Gurney, *Anatolian Studies*, V (1955), pp. 93–111.

17. Cf. *Revue des études anciennes*, XLII (1940), p. 28.

18. A. Caquot, *Semitica*, V (1955), p. 5.

19. *Midrash Tehillin* 80.6.

20. O. Møerkholm, *American Numismatic Society, Museum Notes*, XI (1964), p. 74.

21. H. J. Lenzen (ed.), *Vorläufiger Bericht über die Ausgrabungen in Uruk-Warka*, XVIII (1962), p. 58.

22. E. Benveniste, *RHR*, CVL (1932), p. 175.

23. *Berakoth* 55a.

24. Josephus *Bellum Judaicum* i, 2, 3; Justinus 36.3.

25. *Berakoth* 55a.

26. P. Alfaric, "La Prophétie de Sainte Odile," *Publications de la Faculté des Lettres de l'Université de Strasbourg*, CIV (1946), pp. 128 ff.

27. Gregorius Thaumaturgus *Panegyricus*, section 179 (ed. Koetschau).

28. E. Riess, "Nechepsonis . . . fragmenta," *Philologus, Supplementum* VI (1892), pp. 327 ff.

29. A. K. Grayson and W. G. Lambert, *Journal of Cuneiform Studies*, XVIII (1964).

30. Philo *Vita Mosis* 2. 278.

31. G. B. Hughes, *Journal of Near Eastern Studies*, X (1951), p. 256.

32. Cicero *De Natura Deorum* 3. 5. 11.

33. Plato *Phaedrus* 244.

34. E. Bevan, *Sibyls and Seers* (1927), p. 140.

35. Apollonius Rhodius *Argonautica* ii. 313.

36. Augustinus *Commentarius in Johannem*, Tractatus 35. 8.

37. Augustinus *De Civitate Dei* 10. 9.

38. Augustinus *De Consensu Evangelistarum* 1. 1.

39. Eusebius 9.5.

40. Proclus *Commentarius in Timaeum* II, p. 300 (ed. E. Diehl).

41. H. Dodwell, *Works* (ed. Brookesby) (1723), p. 508, quoted in A. Collins, *A Discourse on Grounds and Reasons of the Christian Religion* (1724), p. 44.

42. Cf. the words of I. Newton quoted p. 128 above. Newton's *Observations upon the Prophecies of Daniel* were first published in 1732. But L. E. Dupin, a learned Roman Catholic scholar, mentions the bipartite division of Daniel as self-evident as early as 1701. See his *Dissertation . . . sur la Bible*, p. 114.

43. H. Corrodi, *Kritische Geschichte des Chiliasmus* (1781), ch. 9, quotes Porphyry (pp. 242 ff., 256) and Marchant (pp. 250, 257). I have not seen his *Freimütige Versuche* (1783).

KOHELETH
(ECCLESIASTES)
or
THE PHILOSOPHY
OF AN
ACQUISITIVE SOCIETY

Koheleth in His Times

IT appears certain that Ecclesiastes was written before the middle of the second century B.C.E.: a fragment dating from the last decades of that century has been discovered among the Dead Sea Scrolls. Ben Sira seems to have been familiar with Ecclesiastes; he wrote his *Ecclesiasticus* ("the little Ecclesiastes," as it was called in the Church) in the first decades of the second century B.C.E.

An even earlier date can be argued. Two Persian terms are used (2:5; 8:11), one of them in the meaning which it had acquired in Greek. *Pardes* (in Greek *paradeisos*) referred to a royal or satrapal enclosed preserve, and is used in this sense in Nehemiah 2:8, in the Song of Songs, and in the Aramaic Book of Enoch, fragments of which have been found among the Dead Sea Scrolls. But Koheleth pairs *gannot* (gardens) with *pardesim*, where he planted "every kind of fruit tree," and in the next clause speaks of the water supply to his "forest sprouting with trees." Thus *pardes* means orchard; that is how *paradeisos* was used by the Greek administration on the Nile as well as on the Persian Gulf in the third century B.C.E. Therefore, Ecclesiastes must have been written in the third century, when Jerusalem and Palestine were under the domination of the Ptolemies, the Macedonian kings of Egypt.

Ecclesiastes, then, is a product of Ptolemaic Jerusalem, and soon became outdated just because it was so up to date at the time of its appearance. The rabbis misunderstood Ecclesiastes, and its Greek translator did not

understand it either. Ecclesiastes has no known antece-
dents or spiritual posterity in Jewish thought. To understand the book we cannot go to linear evidence in the
Bible or to the rabbinic mentality. Koheleth's epigram-
matic brilliance, redolent of Alexandrian witticism, made
his thought susceptible to almost every possible interpretation. Skeptics and pietists alike have found solace in
Ecclesiastes.

Ecclesiastes is an anonymous book. The author does
not give his name, nor does the editor supply it. This
disagrees with the rules of the genre. The sapiential
writer, from Ptah-hotep on, states his name and social
position. The value of the precept is, so to say, propor-
tionate to the authority of the adviser. This is why the
book proclaiming the vanity of human life was second-
arily attributed to King Solomon. As Rabbi Eleazar notes,
if some other man had talked in the same vein, people
would have said that a man who never owned two
perutot (pennies) wants us to believe that he despises the
wealth of the world. Yet the author of Ecclesiastes is
just such an unknown man, whose pretentiousness would
have amused Rabbi Eleazar.

Sapiential writers addressed their counsels to students whom they knew personally and for whom the
precepts were apt. A late Egyptian sage spoke to his
"dear son." Seneca sent his moral letters to Lucilius, his
friend. Koheleth's words, as Jerome observes in his commentary, were not directed to a definite person, but generally to all people. Yet the speaker does not transmit the
trite wisdom that is applicable to everyman's conduct.
He rather puts forward his own person: "I have found,"
"I have seen," and so on. Who is this "I"?

THE CONVOKER

His sayings are the words of "Koheleth," and his editor uses the same generic name with reference to the author of Ecclesiastes. The word means "Convoker." As his editor says (12:9), Koheleth was not only a sage (*hakam*), he also "taught knowledge to the people." A Hebrew sage, like a Greek philosopher or a modern professor, addressed his peers or potential peers, his colleagues and students. The sage did not move in a throng. "Let thy house be a meeting place for sages," said Jose ben Joezer of the second century B.C.E. "Sit in the very dust at their feet, and thirstily drink in their words." Of course, a wise man, as Ben Sira says, will instruct his people, for instance as a political adviser; but Ben Sira was also certain that a man who holds the plow cannot become wise, just as no one not grounded in geometry could pass the gate of Plato's Academy. Koheleth's "words of truth," on the other hand, were addressed to a crowd that gathered around him on the street—a scholar turned haranguer.

Koheleth was not unique in this regard. There were also in his age men like Crates, Menippus, or Bion who sought to teach the right way of life to the common man. Crates read aloud Aristotle's *Exhortation to Philosophy*, written for a king, to a shoemaker stitching in his shop, and said that the cobbler was better qualified for philosophy than the king. Bion persuaded the sailors at Rhodes to put on student's garb and follow him into the gymnasium where professors lectured to their students. This contemporary of Koheleth not only preached in the streets but, like him, was a qualified philosopher who accepted disciples and charged fees for his lectures.

Condemning the useless knowledge of savants, these philosophical preachers of the third century tried passionately to save souls. Stoics, Cynics, and Epicureans, in various degrees, were all pagan salvationists.

But like every street-corner orator, in order to attract attention the wandering philosopher shouted. Like Koheleth he uttered maxims which sounded like paradoxes, easy to remember and difficult to interpret. Salvation for man lay in abandoning conventional values. Accordingly, the preacher restamped the moral currency. In an age of wars and revolutions, exile was the dreaded lot of thousands of Greeks; but the wandering preacher declared to his audience that a "displaced person" might be as happy as a citizen in his own city.

The same is the manner of the Convoker in Jerusalem. He depreciates almost everything that would have been a boon in the eyes of the average Jew. A sage himself, he asserts (2:14) that wisdom and knowledge are ultimately no better than madness and folly. Wealth is useless, pleasure futile, greed senseless, and all toil beneath the sun is worthless (2:11). The traditional wisdom praised hard work, but Koheleth is certain that people toil out of sheer and needless competitiveness (4:4). The Jew, like every man, wanted to leave a good inheritance to his son. Koheleth observes (2:19) that man cannot know whether his heir will be wise or foolish. A proverb noted that man's pleasure lights his face. Koheleth says (7:3) that sorrow is better than laughter. The reassuring periodicity of days and seasons comforts us: when winter comes, spring cannot be far behind. For Koheleth as for a Roman disciple of Greek preachers, the eternal return of sublunar events is wearisome (1:8), *ad nauseam* to use the strong expression of Seneca.

Koheleth may have heard a Greek debater in Palestine. Menippus, a famous freethinker of his time, was from Gadara, on the other side of the Jordan. Yet Wisdom was calling aloud in the noisiest streets of Jerusalem long before the days of Ecclesiastes and Menippus. Surfeited with seeing the world, Koheleth, like Seneca in the letter just cited, stated that there is nothing new. For instance, a wise man would have saved his city, but since he was poor nobody thought of consulting him (9:13–18). This will happen again and again. What need had Koheleth of learning from Aristotle to avoid the extremes; what need of reading books to speak of the decrepitude of old age and to remind us that you cannot take money with you into the grave?

VANITY, LUCK, AND VIRTUE

Thus at first blush, Koheleth's thought agrees with the Greek philosophical sermon. Do you wish to be of good cheer? Do not take delight in vain things. Koheleth's *hebel*, which we render "vanity" following the Old Latin versions of Ecclesiastes, properly means "vapor." Greek contemporaries of the Hebrew Convoker called the same conceits "smoke" (*typhos*). All current opinion was just smoke, and man, disdaining appearances, must make his way to the Truth.

Yet the meaning of the Truth was not the same for the Preacher in Jerusalem and for the Greek Convokers. For the Greeks, the vanity of life proved that man ought to abandon the pleasures, and so on. Sickness and even death itself were external and for this reason matters of indifference. From such domination man ought to be free. When the sole slave of Diogenes ran away, the philosopher remarked: "If Manes can live without Diogenes, it would be strange that Diogenes should not be of good cheer without Manes." Nothing had value but inner freedom; the only striving worth-while was to become captain of one's own soul. Thus, absence of emotional troubles, the attainment of peace of mind, was the goal of the sage. Even Epicurus, who considered pleasure the only aim of life and pain the only absolute evil, asserted that a wise man might be happy on the rack by the supremacy of his inward life over things external.

The Greek philosophers started from the premise that men were pawns in the hands of capricious forces. The carefree lords of Mount Olympus did not care a straw for unhappy mortals, and it was dangerous to be too happy. From Heraclitus down to a slave in a comedy of Menander, the Greeks repeated that man's character is his destiny. In the Classical Age, however, man could trust his city gods, bribing them, as Plato says, by sacrifices, civic virtues, and so on. But the mobility of the Greeks of the third century made protection by city gods in large measure illusory. A man, say of Labranda, who migrated to Philadelphia, in Egypt, in the time of Koheleth, would have found a temple of Zeus of Labranda in his new settlement. But in Egypt what was the patron saint of Labranda? Just one of innumerable and indistinguishable idols who peopled the country of the Nile. And again, if Zeus of Labranda could not make man's life secure in his own city, how would he protect him in a land far away? The late Egyptian Wisdom Book well expresses this parochial mentality: the god of a community gives life and death, but abroad his greatness is known no more.

Thus, in the age of Alexander and after, Luck (*Tyche*) became man's deity, even if she was worshiped with insults. It is very significant that it was Fortuna who became the divine projection and celestial protector of new Hellenistic cities: Luck of Antioch, Luck of Dura-Europos. To this world of Chance, the Stoics brought the discovery of Providence (or Fate, also called Zeus, or Nature), the deity ruling the universe through causal connection of happenings. If man is attuned to the cosmic order, he will be happy, provided the outward misfortunes are understood to be in themselves unimportant. Whatever does no moral harm cannot be evil.

As to the external circumstances of his life, willingly or unwillingly man had to follow the route imposed by Fate. No symbol of human life was more popular in the Hellenistic philosophy than the Actor playing well whatever part is assigned to him by the divine playwright and producer. "Virtue suffices for living well."

The virtuous pagan stood alone. In a world grounded on the rock of the Covenant the Jew was not alone. Through the promises given to the Patriarchs, the Jew was partner in the pact with Providence. All misfortunes of the Chosen People, or of any son of Israel, were due to their own sins. "For the Lord loves justice and forsakes not His saints." In the framework of covenanted faith theodicy was superfluous. Even Job's sufferings were, as we are told in advance, only a test of his faith. Thus, the complaints against the agency of Providence, the answers of his friends, and God's final retort are a rhetorical joust. The question of the book is not whether God is just but how Job, who had feared God and shunned evil, will stand his test. And with Job (19:25), the Jew exclaimed: "I know that my Redeemer lives."

Koheleth is Job who failed in the test. Perhaps he was tried in a wrong way, with rewards. His thesis is that all is vanity. How can all be vain, Jerome will ask, if God found His creation good? And Augustine, playing on the words of his Latin Bible, will say that all is vain for vain men.

To understand Koheleth and his aphoristic style let us first summarize his discursive and repetitious reasoning. All is vain for two reasons. First, death ends all. Koheleth disproves possible objections. The end is unrelated to man's deserts, and one fate will meet both the righteous and the wicked. There is no survival, neither personal in the abode of the dead, nor through children. Remembrance was the supreme hope of a righteous man, in Jerusalem as in Athens. But for Koheleth the memory of all the dead, their love, their hatred, and their envy ultimately perish. Second: unchangeable yet unpredictable fate has no relation to man's deeds. The wicked man may prosper (7:15)—and "there are upright men who are requited according to the conduct of scoundrels" (8:14). And because death renders the success illusory, "The race is not won by the swift, nor the battle by the valiant" (9:11).

These proofs of the futility of life were neither new nor necessarily persuasive. The Psalmist (102:11) and the Greek poet Pindar had declared before Koheleth that man's life is just a shadow. An ancient Babylonian poet had already complained that the skulls of the dead did not tell whether in life a man had been just, or an evildoer. Ben Sira no less than Koheleth emphasized the truth that death is with all flesh, from man to beast. That man proposes but God disposes was a truism, repeated by all wise men, from the Egyptian Ptah-hotep in the third millennium B.C.E. to King Agur of Proverbs and the Greek poet Semonides of Amorgos. The author of the Demotic sapiential book was grieved, like Koheleth, that the deity hides the future from man, that the length of life assigned to man is unrelated to his deserts, that Fate and Luck determine a human life. Yet both came from the deity. The deity was omnipotent and His will inscrutable. The Egyptian sage, however, inferred from this fact that man ought to trust God. His book ends on this note: it is the reward of the wise man that God's eye watches over him, while the heart of the fool does not know God.

ELOHIM

In contrast to the "fools," Koheleth knew that everything depends on the will of God. God predestined everything, even man's capacity to enjoy his riches. But Koheleth's *Elohim* was an unpredictable, morally neutral being, beyond good and evil. Man is in the hand of God, but *Elohim* goes His way regardless of man. For Koheleth God was as arbitrary and fickle as Luck, which was worshiped by the common man in Greece. But Luck changed, while Koheleth's *Elohim* was as ineluctable as the Fate of the philosophers. In the all-seeing presence of his *Elohim*, Koheleth felt, to use his simile (13:12), like a fish caught in a net. The Sage of Jerusalem had to advise men how to adjust their lives to the vanity of Life. Accordingly, he collected some miscellaneous admonitions which fill up a great part of his book, for use in the uncertainty of the future. For instance, he reminded his hearers after Solomon (Prov. 26:27) that he who digs a pit shall fall into it (10:8). He warned against failing to fulfill a vow (5:4) and against bad temper (7:9). In Proverbs it is said, "Fear the Lord and the king" (24:21). Koheleth has the same attitude toward both supernatural and earthly authority. Who can say to either: "What doest thou?" (8:4)? For the king, however, the hour of doom will come. The arbitrary rule of *Elohim* is deathless, and for Koheleth the traditional precept to "fear God" means to be on guard against *Elohim*.

Epicurus would prefer the vulgar notion of personal gods to "slavery" under the stoic Necessity. The Stoics, the author of the Demotic Wisdom, and the Solomon of Proverbs all cheerfully accepted the divine government of the world because they trusted in the wisdom and kindness of Providence. "Whom the Lord loves He reproves even as a father the son in whom he delights" (Prov. 3:12). But Koheleth has lost this child's faith and trust. As a Sage of Jerusalem, versed in the Torah and in a sapiential literature based on belief in Providence, how did Koheleth arrive at his image of *Elohim?* We do not know the anonymous author, nor can we date him exactly. We cannot uncover his motives. But the intellectual reasons for his quarrel with God are still discernible in his book.

Like Greek wandering preachers and perhaps in imitation of them, Koheleth proclaimed the emptiness of conventional values. But the criticism of life, which for the Greeks affected only external things, came in the covenanted universe of the Jew to touch God Himself, who had created and governed the world. Aristotle said, and the Greeks of Koheleth's age believed, that these external things, be they wealth or childlessness, were governed by Chance. But for a Jew, if man was alone in this world of Chance, where was the God of Abraham, Isaac, and Jacob? The dichotomy of soul and body which was at the base of Greek philosophical thought remained alien to the Jew, so alien that he could not conceive of an afterlife except as resurrection. Thus for the Jewish sage the discovery of the vanity of the world was not a step to liberation but a confession of despair. For Koheleth, as he says himself (9:3), the absence of retributive justice—shrugged off by a contemporary Greek dissenter—was the basic evil of all that happened under the sun. The Hebrew protest against Providence, from Job to Elisha ben Abuya, the arch-heretic of the rabbinic age, is formulated by Malachi (2:17): "Where is the God

of Justice?" The Jews, following the Greeks, later saved
the mystery of man's fate in this world by promising
justice triumphant in the world that is to come. When
the author of the *Wisdom of Solomon,* in the age of
Philo and Hillel, set himself to refute the ungodly who
thought as Koheleth that our life is the passing of a
shadow, he spoke of a restoration of the divine kingdom
in the future.

Similarly, the assertion of the vanity of fame or wisdom, and other elements of Koheleth's nihilism (which
in a Greek's mouth would be an almost ascetic condemnation of worldly advantages), inevitably destroyed
the morality based on the traditional notion of divine
governance of the world. If life was transient and the
future unforeseeable, the only wise rule of conduct was
to enjoy one's worldly goods and make the most of the
present. Thus, paradoxically, the criticism of conventional views led not to stoic negation but to enjoyment
as the sole tangible value.

The talmudic teachers understood that all the wisdom of Koheleth is summarized in his appeal to cheer
the heart in the days of its prime. One rabbi heard the
voice of evil desire in these words of Ecclesiastes. Another, more charitably and more wisely, said that good
desire speaks here. In fact, Koheleth echoed the primeval
and eternal voice of the frightened man trying to fool
Death. From the Sumerian King Gilgamesh down to
Horace and an Egyptian priest contemporary with Cleopatra, the intense contemplation of pallid Death called
forth the same watchword: *carpe diem.* The Sage of
Jerusalem feared Death and repeatedly denied a survival
after death. If a live dog is better than a dead lion (9:4),
there is no good for a mortal man under the sun, except
to eat, drink, and be merry. The epitaph of Sardanapalus,
the legendary last king of Nineveh, who for the Greeks

became the prototype of profligacy, is strangely consonant with the voice of the Sage of Jerusalem. Allegedly translated from "Chaldean" it proclaims: "Knowing for certain that you are mortal, lift up your heart, enjoy feasting. . . . I still have what I ate, and what I indulged in and what pleasures of love I experienced—but my famous and numberless treasures have been left behind."

Yet Koheleth was no pleasure seeker. Voluptuaries brought images of death into banquets to sharpen the appetite for earthly joys. Koheleth (7:2) advises his hearers to go to the house of mourning rather than to a house of feasting, in order to learn the inevitable end of human life. He also speaks against sloth, condemns carousing, warns against women, and praises docility and patience. His pleasures are selfish because he is not a Greek philosopher but a man of traditional prudence called upon to give practical counsels which are universally valid. He does not address sages or saints. He admonishes the man in the street that pursuit of money is as foolish as revelry or wisdom. The openhandedness so prized by the Greeks is outside the purview of his practical wisdom. He does not recommend charity, as do his biblical models, on the ground that it is pleasing to God; nor does he praise friendship, as the Greeks did. Suspicious of the future, he thinks of reducing the risks. Do kindness to many people, give a portion to seven or eight men. One of your beneficiaries may by chance show himself grateful if misfortune befalls you. "Woe betide him who is alone and falls with no companion to raise him" (4:10). In the time of Koheleth high priests and probably other magnates of Jerusalem erected public buildings, which served the people in the Greek manner. To Koheleth the idea of public service is alien; the government for him is tyrannical, and there is no word in Ecclesiastes on man's duties to his fellow men.

The contradictions in Ecclesiastes, already noted by rabbinic commentators, are a manifestation of the sober attitude of the Sage of Jerusalem. The essential quality of the book is explained neither by the tradition nor by the parallel sayings of Ecclesiastes. It is a religious book. Of its 222 verses, 122 are quoted in rabbinic sources. Koheleth is a God-fearing man who is certain that we cannot enjoy the pleasures of the life he celebrates except by God's grace, or rather, upon *Elohim's* whim. Many found in Ecclesiastes, as Jerome tells us, an appeal to pleasure. Yet Koheleth, who knows that it is pleasant for the eyes to behold the sun, sees the permanence of nature as a foil to the transitoriness of human life. Hence Jerome could find in Ecclesiastes an appeal to asceticism.

So Koheleth's counsel is as universal as life and as timeless as death. His vision transcends and embraces the opposites of his interpreters. The Synagogue wisely understood this despairing book as an appeal to happiness. It is read in the Sukkot week, "the season of rejoicing." Koheleth, at the conclusion of the debate, teaches that the whole duty of man is to "fear God, and keep His commandments" (12:13).

Ecclesiastes could have been written only by a devout Jew who had discovered that there was no Providence, and that he was alone in a world foreign to him. Koheleth made this discovery because he was born into an age of enlightenment. This age was ushered in by a startling declaration of Aristotle, made when Alexander was conquering the East, that we ought not to follow those who say that men should have thoughts which befit mortals. Through the life of the intellect, akin to the divine, we should strive to achieve deathlessness. Some decades later, a character in an Attic comedy boasted, "The Intellect is God in every one of us."

Koheleth lived in the age when Eratosthenes exhibited a mechanical device for the duplication of the cube, and Archimedes, like a god of Plato, to borrow Cicero's pertinent words, rotated a sphere reproducing the movements of the starry heavens. A Greek settler in Egypt invented a machine which he believed would make up for the deficiencies of the Nile, and in distant Nubia the native king, infected by Greek rationalism, overthrew the government of priests. "Give me a spot on which to stand, and I will move the earth," said Archimedes.

In Jerusalem, Koheleth is not satisfied with modifying the traditional wisdom. For the first time in Jewish sapiential literature, so far as is known (except for Prov. 24:32), the Sage gives precedence to his "I." The first person of the verb is not sufficient. He adds the pronoun *ani*, though it is emphatic or pleonastic. For the first time in Hebrew writings the term *darash* is used by Koheleth (1:3) in the sense of investigating a problem—a meaning which was later to become common in the rabbinic schools. Again and again Koheleth stresses his personal experience of life. For the first time in Jerusalem, as far as we know, a man seeks to find out the secret of God's causing what happens under the sun (8:17). Koheleth conducts a psychological experiment (2:1). He essays the three types of life as classified by the Greek philosophers—pleasure, contemplation, and action—and he finds all three wanting.

The problem with which Koheleth struggled was the problem of all intellectuals of his time: is there an aim to life? Greek philosophers were ready to declare what the highest good is, and how the Deity governs the world. But man was the beginning and end of the dis-

cussions of the Greeks. The schools debated the question
of why the wicked prospered, but those who denied divine retribution nevertheless concurred that it was impossible to live happily without living wisely and justly.

But the God of Israel could not be disposed of so
easily. Koheleth took the logomachy seriously. In this
early period of Greek influence sages of Jerusalem did
not yet know how to handle the new intellectual tools
safely. Koheleth assumed that to be happy man must
obtain rational understanding of God's ways. Aiming so
high, he went beyond the aspirations of the Greek philosophers, but intellectual audacity was in the air. Men
believed that they were playthings of Fortune, but also
that they might find out the schedule of events. Astrology
began its conquest of the Greek mind in this age of enlightenment. Koheleth does not mention astrology, but
he stresses that wisdom is vain because it cannot discover
the scheme (*heshbon*) of God in preordaining events
(7:25). "Who can tell a man what the future holds for
him under the sun?" (6:11).

Koheleth wanted the very certainty he had lost in
searching to know what profit man has from all his toil
under the sun. But if you deny Providence in this life
and survival in afterlife, you are bound to fall in with
the hedonist's egotism. We are on leave from Death to
visit the festival of Life. He who enjoys it most will de-
part having got the most out of it. No less a man than
Augustine confessed that he would have given the prize
to Epicurus in the contest about the aim of life if he did
not believe in the survival of the soul and the profits of
meritorious deeds.

The despair of Koheleth is that he cannot be a hedonist. If like him you consider man as an isolated being
(another trait of early Hellenistic mentality), and if you
have the courage never to rest until you have found the

rock on which to base your answer to the riddle of life, and if, therefore, the good is to make the most of life—then you must conclude that life is not worth living, since life is fleeting. "Ecclesiastes shows that man without God is in total ignorance and inevitable wretchedness. For to have wishes but no power is to be wretched. He wishes to be happy and assured of some truth, and yet he can neither know nor desire not to know. He cannot even doubt" (Pascal).

Not eudaemonism but, as pious and penetrating commentators of old realized, his intellectual boldness was Koheleth's undoing. "Going beyond the permissible," as Jerome says, Koheleth wanted to understand the ways of God. This was an evil task given to men by God: to investigate through wisdom everything that is done beneath the heavens. For increased knowledge means increased pain (1:13–18).

Milton shows the Fallen Angels reasoning high "of Providence, Foreknowledge, Will and Fate . . . Vain Wisdom all, and false Philosophy." There is something of a Fallen Angel in the author of Ecclesiastes. The optimistic rationalism of the Hellenistic enlightenment began to wane, however, toward the end of the third century. The deaths of Archimedes (212 B.C.E.) and of Chrysippus (206 B.C.E.) marked the end of an intellectual epoch. By the middle of the second century, the great astronomer Hipparchus of Nicaea believed in astrology. This does not mean, of course, that there were no men of old-fashioned piety in the third century (the historian Timaeus was one) or that everybody became anti-rationalist in the second century (Polybius did not) but the trend is unmistakable.

In Jerusalem, Koheleth's boldness was succeeded by Ben Sira's humility. "Thou hast no need of the things that are hidden." The reference is to the word of the

Torah (Deut. 29:29) that the hidden things belong to the Lord. The weakness of Koheleth's philosophical position was that he offered no philosophy but simply opposed the experience of a skeptic to the orthodox system of morality. Ben Sira, who, we assume, knew Ecclesiastes, could again emphatically affirm that here, on earth, the reward shall not fail the righteous. He, too, appealed to experience: a good wife is given to him who fears the Lord. He could scoff at the light-minded hedonists who believed that God would not notice their misdeeds, and reminded the evildoer that the day of wrath, if sometimes delayed, is inescapable. Asserting that man should limit his desire for knowledge, Ben Sira added that hypotheses lead many astray. Did he have in mind the men who were soon going to ask the Syrian king to reform the faith of their fathers?

It is surprising that the lonely book of the sad sage of Ptolemaic Jerusalem survived. Yet the Sadducees, like Koheleth, denied divine Providence. On the other hand, the brilliance of his style must have touched artistic chords in even the most orthodox souls. The book was recognized as a classic immediately and was studied in the schools. At that time, the name of Solomon affixed to the book definitely masked the author. As the rabbis so nicely put it, Ecclesiastes was written by the disillusioned king at the end of his long life.

The Uses of Wealth

Koheleth still speaks to us today. But it was to his contemporaries in Ptolemaic Jerusalem that he addressed the advice: "Go, eat your bread in gladness and drink your wine in joy" (9:7). Koheleth has not in mind the laborer who sleeps sweetly whether he eats little or much (5:12). Koheleth speaks rather to the affluent whose sleep is troubled by worry about their abundant resources (5:11). A large part of his slim scroll deals with the exertion of acquisition. He repeats often (1:3; 2:11; 2:24; 3:9; 3:13; 3:22; 5:14–17; 8:15; 9:9) that profit making in itself is futile (the term *amal* here means not toil, but its fruit, profit, as Jerome and Samuel ben Meir [c. 1080–1160] and H. L. Ginsberg have demonstrated). The idea was not new. The sage of the Proverbs (23:4) advises his reader not to weary himself to be rich since wealth is fleeting. What is surprising is Koheleth's insistence that pleasure is the sole good which acquisitive labor may bring to a money-maker. The classical moralists in the Orient as well as in Greece reminded the affluent man to expend riches on goods, friends, and strangers. Koheleth preaches to him not to forget himself. He thus enters the debate on the right use of wealth, a question which occupied the minds of Greek philosophers and, as Greek comedy shows, bothered the average man in the age of Koheleth.

The sharp-eyed Aristotle, on the eve of Alexander's conquest of Asia, distinguished between two forms of acquisition. Domestic management (*oikonomike*), which was typical of the classical Greek city, represents acquisition for consumption, to provide for livelihood. "Business" (*chremastike*), on the other hand, is based on the notion that there is no limit to the acquisition of riches. This accumulative art of money-making became a determinant feature of the Hellenistic age.

In the poor country of Greece the only practical means for acquiring wealth were industry and intelligence. After Alexander's conquest, the Greeks in the Orient brought with them efficiency, a taste for innovations, exact accounting, and a polite but unadorned style of business letters. As usual in a colonial country, they brought with them limitless greed, which Plato in his day regarded as Levantine. The Oriental idea was that the deity gives riches to a good man so that he may have no further cares. On an Egyptian tomb, built shortly before the Ptolemean rule, we can see the master resting in the shade while his men work for him in the sun. Greed, competition, and the unlimited resources of the new world created the type of businessman who had no time or desire for *dolce far niente*. Zenon, a business agent in the time of Koheleth, has left us his archives. His business was his life. "Hurry up" is the refrain of his correspondence. He was a type: "You are busy with so many affairs, you harass and bewilder yourself . . . you undergo all kinds of disagreeable things, and you have no benefit of it," says a Hellenistic philosopher to the seeker of riches. In the Athens of the fifth century, the debtor suffered from sleepless nights. In Hellenistic Athens it was the rich man who could not sleep for worry about his business affairs.

THE NEW CLASS

Toil, not inherited wealth, now brought affluence; and one who boasted but had no bread was despised. In Proverbs (10:4) the diligent man is contrasted to the slothful one; another saying (28:22) warns against the desire to get rich quickly. Ben Sira in his patchwork manner twists both proverbs together. Under his hand the old-fashioned wisdom of husbandry is transformed into advice against multiplying business ventures. And he contrasts the poor man raised up by God with one who tries to get rich by "laboring, toiling, and running." But the same Ben Sira (42:7) also traces the portrait of a paragon of the new mercantile class, who is engaged in many tasks and works hard. He is not ashamed of the Torah, nor of justice, nor of reckoning with a partner in tax-underwriting and in the caravan trade, of returning the inheritance of a business partner, of exactness in weighing and measuring. He is also not ashamed of correcting children and slaves, nor of profiting from traffic. The most famous man of the new business class in Jerusalem was the tax-contractor Joseph, who amassed an enormous fortune in the last decades of the third century. His biographer, Flavius Josephus, ascribes to Joseph the virtues of Poor Richard. Joseph became wealthy "by working hard and controlling his desires." His son and heir Hyrcanus was no less industrious. But Hyrcanus' brothers, who opposed him, lacked "the love of work." When Hyrcanus was later deprived of power and relegated to the Transjordan, he did not waste time. He again started to get rich, this time by the most ancient means: war and plunder.

The Greek intellectuals, who more or less consciously

endeavored to preserve the ideal of a classical city (*polis*) in a world dominated by great kings and immense empires, disliked the new businessman. A *polis* was no place for nabobs. Its existence depended on class equilibrium. Looking backward, the philosophers preached the classical ideal of freedom from business of all kinds. They assumed that their hearers belonged to the leisured class of hereditary gentlemen-farmers, or that the student was an intellectual for whom it sufficed to live on plain bread and water, as Epicurus said. It was right for a man to acquire the means necessary to his livelihood, but to seek more was greed. Though they were busy collecting fees (Epicurus spoke of "tribute" owed him by his adherents, and taxed them regularly), their social theory was still geared to a static type of society, where the farmer and the craftsman were but little removed in status from their workmen. Yet the philosopher Cleanthes had to work during the night in a mill to be able to study in the school of Zeno. In fact, one philosopher complained that most of the students abandoned their training early because of the necessity of earning a living.

Nevertheless, toward the middle of the third century, by proclaiming the principle of living in conformity with Nature which has given us the instinct of self-preservation, the Stoics allowed a gentleman to strive for health, riches, and other worldly goods. Chrysippus, a contemporary of Koheleth, spoke at length of the habit pattern of men engaged in the accumulation, safeguarding and spending of wealth. The Stoics discussed questions of the new business ethics, for instance whether a moral man ought to disclose the hidden defects of his merchandise to the buyer. Diogenes of Seleucia, apostle of free enterprise, argued that not to tell does not mean to conceal. The opposite view impairs the rights attendant on property ownership. "What kind of society is it where no one shall have anything of his own?" Profit was no longer "filthy." In the dialogue "Hipparchus," written in the first decades of the third century and later wrongly ascribed to Plato, Socrates tries to find out what is "sordid covetousness," but after discarding the notion that it is what the gentleman would not do to make profit, he decides finally that all gains are good because all men are greedy for some good.

Nevertheless, Greek intellectuals of the third century still asserted that a man who dedicated his life to the accumulation of wealth was a fool. For the Stoics, money was neither good nor evil. The Cynics praised the man who worked for his daily maintenance, and they continued to regard money as the root of all evil. In Alexandria, the business center of the Hellenistic world, the literati celebrated the blessings of honest and happy poverty. The philosophers freely gave advice praising frugality and modesty. For the man in the street, who was hardly satisfied with the precept that at a time of need one should borrow from himself by eating less, Epicurus rationalized and justified the common-sense belief that acquisition of riches makes sense only as a means to a good living, and for nothing else. The Epicureans, though they condemned greed, reinstated pleasure. They approved of the possession of riches and taught how "to make the use of wealth painless and the enjoyment it gives perfect." For the man in the street, Epicurus' gospel was that of bodily satisfaction. As a cook says in an Athenian comedy, "Epicurus intensified pleasure, he chewed carefully, he alone knew the nature of good."

For the Stoics, on the other hand, "good men" were not only pitiless; they were also austere, and neither had themselves an appetite for pleasure, nor tolerated this inclination in others. As at other periods of the early stages of capital accumulation, in Victorian England no less than in Stalin's Russia, pleasure which distracts from work was considered the Enemy. The panegyrist of the publican Joseph, mentioned above, tells of the dangerous passion of his hero for a dancing girl of King Ptolemy. But a brother of Joseph, by using the deception practiced by Laban on Jacob, marries his daughter to the tax-farmer.

FROM FRUGALITY TO LUXURY

In classical Greece, with its limited means of acquisition, "filthy lucre" was exemplified in such deals as selling watered-down wine to a friend, or using another's oil in a bathhouse. This is rather the greed of a miser. In the early Hellenistic age, stinginess was no longer a sign of avarice, but of dotage and incompetence. Joseph and Hyrcanus were spendthrifts. They amassed fortunes by throwing money around in gifts and bribes. This was not only the best manner to win friends but, in the opinion of envious contemporaries, the best way to share one's wealth with one's fellow man.

Hellenistic literature abounds in attacks against the parsimonious millionaire. Moralists described how in the latter's soul the demon of pleasure struggles with and succumbs to the demon of money-loving. The wealthy were admonished that the test of riches is in their use. In classical Greece, Tantalus, unable to quench his thirst, was a symbol of greed. In the Hellenistic preaching, he became a symbol of stinginess. In Vergil's hell there are not robber barons but niggardly millionaires: *divitiis soli incubere repertis nec partem posuere suis*.

Investment may be preferable economically to outlay for ostentatious consumption. But a free-spending

Maecenas was not only aesthetically more pleasing than a tight-fisted monopolist; he was also a potential bene-factor. The poor man could at least take delight in the odor coming from the kitchen of his wealthy neighbor. Grave historians could continue to explain the fall of rulers and nations by their luxurious living (*tryphe*). But in the popular usage the word was a term of praise. The "Garden of Eden" is "Garden of *Tryphe*" in the Greek Bible, and the kings, from Ptolemy III on, readily accepted the nickname "Tryphon."

In the rocky land of Judaea where riding a horse was a mark of wealth (10:7) but shredded straw was used as fodder, a neighbor who got rich quickly was a sore in the public eye. When poor men had to huddle together to keep warm in the winter night—"how can he who is alone get warm?" (4:11)—the dominion of wealth was both provocative and overwhelming. "Don't revile a king even among your intimates; don't revile a rich man even in your bedchamber. For a bird of the air may carry the utterance" (10:20).

Old-fashioned people disliked the new ways of the Greeks and of the publicans. Koheleth speaks disdainfully (10:7) of slaves who, becoming rich, mount horses, and it is with sorrow that he sees impoverished nobles who walk on foot like slaves. According to Flavius Josephus, it was a slave who as business agent managed the fortune of the tax-farmer Joseph in Alexandria, which was said to amount to three thousand talents (about four and a half millions of gold dollars) and who was personally known to the Ptolemaic king. But Koheleth was behind the times. He invested in land only and stored up his riches in gold and silver (2:5,8), without adventures in trade or tax-farming.

He speaks of the new businessman who day and night labors with wisdom and industry (again these newfangled

Greek notions). His days are painful, and even in the
night his heart takes no rest. His eyes are never satisfied
with riches, and he never pauses to ask himself why he
deprives his soul of pleasures. Yet the riches may get lost
in business ventures. What profit from his toil has he
who labored for wind, and ate his bread in vexation and
trouble? Or the businessman may die suddenly (from a
heart attack, perhaps), leaving all the fruit of his toil to
an heir who may not even be his son or brother. "All
labor and skillful enterprise come from envy of each other
—another futility and pursuit of wind" (4:4; cf. 2:21;
4:5–8; 5:11–16).

A generation later, Ben Sira in turn depicts the rich
man who first labors to gain wealth and then cannot sleep
for anxiety about it. How different are these business-
men of Hellenistic Jerusalem from her noble rulers in
the days of Isaiah (22:13), who ate flesh and drank wine
"for tomorrow we shall die."

THE ENJOYMENT OF WEALTH

Koheleth is a sage who in an age of investment
teaches not dissipation, but the enjoyment of wealth. Addressing affluent hearers, his theme is the meaning of
toil for the rich man. He asks him not, as the Greek
philosophers did, to share the wealth with others, but to
share it with his own body—for tomorrow we shall die.
If you have wealth, says Ben Sira, echoing Koheleth, be
good to yourself, because there is no pleasure in Hades.

The arrogant grandees and adventurous capitalists
spoken of by Koheleth and Ben Sira are buried in oblivion. The Maccabean tempest overthrew the entire
class, which was suspect of unorthodoxy. The new lead-
ers were no less rapacious, but godly. But the Trans-

jordanian seat of the above-mentioned tax-farmer Hyrcanus has been partly preserved, and twenty-three centuries later we can still visualize the style of life of the nabobs whom Koheleth admonished in his time.

The place, now called "the prince's cliff" ('Araq el-Emir), is situated twelve miles east of the Jordan, and about ten miles northwest of Hesbon. "Tyrus" (probably from the Aramaic *tur*ᶜ, hill), as the manor was called, consisted of several structures. Two tiers of chambers and corridors tunneled into a precipitous cliff about five hundred meters long and over twenty-five meters high probably served as living quarters for Hyrcanus' retainers and as a place of refuge against an enemy force. One of these caves in the upper tier, accessible by a ramp, had a gallery thirty meters long, about six meters wide, and about four meters high, which was used for horses. This stable had mangers for more than a hundred horses. The name "Tobiah" is inscribed in Aramaic script to the right of the entrance to a cave. The date of the inscription is uncertain. It is assigned to the beginning of the fifth century B.C.E., although Josephus ascribes the tunneling of the cliff to Hyrcanus. Some six hundred meters to the south Hyrcanus built the edifice which was later admiringly described by Josephus. In an artificial lake fed by an aqueduct bringing water from a perennial stream high in the mountains, a raised earthen platform supported an oblong building (thirty-seven meters by eighteen-and-one-half meters) of enormous white stones. A stairway led to a tower. The entrance was adorned by a porch of the latest Alexandrian fashion, of two Corinthian columns between two pilasters. A frieze of enormous lions (each animal three meters long and two meters high) in relief ran below the cornice across the façade of the building. The pillars in the interior bore capitals of eagles and bulls' heads in the Persian style. The remains of an enormous winged sphinx, which probably guarded the edifice, again evinces the Graeco-Egyptian style. Josephus speaks of artificial landscaping, of terraces and gardens laid out around the central edifice.

The elaborate system of aqueducts and drains brought water from the perennial stream (Wadi es-Sir) up to the park and to the deep and wide artificial lake around the castle. (An ancient aqueduct still supplies water to the Arab village of Araq some three hundred meters above Wadi es-Sir). A fountain with a feline animal as a waterspout has been discovered at a corner of the central building. A channel within the building brought (and can still bring) water to the animal's spout.

This seignoral residence reminds us of Koheleth. A generation before Hyrcanus, Koheleth also built houses for himself, made gardens and orchards and pools of water.

THE SCROLL OF ESTHER

ESTHER

or

ESTHER AND MORDECAI

The Double Plot

THE Scroll of Esther narrates how the plan to slay all
the Jews in the Persian Empire was thwarted by a providential interposition, how the Jews in self-defense anni-
hilated their enemies, and how a feast of deliverance was
instituted. This feast, Purim, is still celebrated by the
Jews.

The straightforward style of the narrative gives it
the appearance of a factual report. An ancient Christian
commentator, however, makes us realize the complexity
of the biblical book:[1] he asks why the Book of Esther
bears her name although the principal character in the
story is Mordecai. (In fact, in II Maccabees 15:36 Purim
is called "the day of Mordecai.") His answer is that she
was a queen and ready to sacrifice her life for her people. The commentator reproduces the rabbinical question and answer of which only the latter has been preserved in Jewish tradition. After saying that three things
are called after Moses, the anonymous source of the
Midrash on Exodus 30:4 adds: "and similarly Esther
risked her life for Israel, and they [some things] were
called after her and it is written: to make supplication
before him [the king] for her people" (Esther 4:8).

As often in ancient interpretations of venerable
texts, be it Bible or Homer, it is not the solution but the
problem posed which is important. The ancient readers
read seriously and took their texts seriously. Their ear
heard every dissonance. The problem of the title of the
Book of Esther, once formulated, makes the structure of

this book evident. It has two heroes because it has two plots. In the first, Esther, a Jewess, becomes a Persian queen, but the enmity of Haman, the king's vizir, endangers her position and life. She succeeds in saving herself and her people and in bringing Haman to the gallows. In the second, Mordecai, a Jewish courtier, is hated by the vizir Haman. The latter prepares the gallows for his enemy but by accident the king discovers Mordecai's past services and orders Haman to honor his rival. In other words, the book has two heroes and two plots, but the villain is the same in both. The author combined two plots and two tales with extraordinary skill, but some stitches are apparent. Thus, though both the king (6:10) and Haman (5:13; 6:13) know that Mordecai is a Jew, they remain ignorant of the race of Esther, who is the cousin and adopted daughter of Mordecai.

Mordecai's Pride

Let us first examine Mordecai's story. The theme is taken from Oriental court life and from the Oriental novel. It is the struggle between the vizir who is established in royal favor and a new dashing courtier, a man from nowhere who by his cleverness and by chance outwits the vizir and in turn becomes the favorite of the king. The last story of the Arabian Nights tells how Marouf, a cobbler of Cairo, lying and scheming, becomes a son-in-law of the khalif; how the khalif's vizir warns his master and for a time succeeds in his evil designs; and

A reconstruction of the Persian Palace at Susa, by M. Pillet, the architect of the French excavations there. Although somewhat fanciful, it gives an idea of how the palace might have looked. In the foreground, the gate where Mordecai sat as royal courtier. In the background, the marble audience hall. Lower buildings, in brick, contained the king's private apartments, the harem, service quarters, etc.

Courtesy of Dura-Europos Publications

Fresco in the Dura-Europos synagogue, painted c. 245 C.E.
Left: Mordecai, in regal Iranian garments, rides a white
steed, led by Haman, dressed as a stable boy. Right:
Ahasuerus and Esther (identified by Aramaic inscriptions)
occupy the throne, attended by courtiers. In the center,
four bystanders.

how at the end, with the help of his wife the princess, Marouf overthrows the vizir.

We can trace the theme back at least to the seventh century B.C.E. An Aramaic book, already read in the fifth century by the Jews at Elephantine, at the southern end of Egypt, and which became extremely popular later (its hero appears on a Roman mosaic in Germany), tells the story of Achiqar. From a Babylonian text composed in 171 B.C.E. we now know that "Ahuqar" was the name given by the Arameans to Aba'enlidarli, a Babylonian who was the "sage" at the court of Esarhaddon of Assyria (680–69).[2] In the present Aramaic version he is placed for some reason under Sennacherib (704–681). Chief minister of the Assyrian king, Achiqar is brought down by the intrigues of his nephew Nadab. Condemned to death, he is saved by his executioner whom he had obliged on some occasion; he remains hidden in the dungeon and reappears when the king is in dire need of his wisdom. His nephew is put into the same dungeon, where he dies.

There are numerous variations on this popular theme. It is used twice in the cycle of Daniel's tales (ch. 3, 6). The theme charmed the Christians in the Middle Ages no less than the Arabs listening to the stories of Scheherezade, and it passed into folklore: a falsely accused minister reinstates himself by his cleverness, a variant also known from Persian sources.[3] The folk tale mirrored life. At every court, from the palace of Esarhaddon to the White House, the best way of advancement is to trip up one's chief. The difficulty for the inventor of Mordecai's story was how to make his rise to power attractive to the hearer, who generally does not like upstarts. Of course the reader can be amused by a knave like Marouf, but the tale of Mordecai was for its author not a story of the Arabian Nights, but a new example of divine favor to the Chosen People.

Mordecai is a courtier. He lives in the royal citadel at Susa and sits, like Daniel before him (Dan. 2:49), "in the king's gate" (2:21; 6:10; 6:12), that is, at the entrance to the royal palace where the officials received petitioners and dealt with government business. In Greek sources the term "the Royal Gate" means the court of the Persian king. For a similar reason, the government of Turkish Sultans was known in Europe as "the Sublime Porte." The visitor at Persepolis, one of the capitals of the ancient Persian Empire, having passed the double gate of the palace, can still sit on the stone benches once used in the days of Ahasuerus by Mordecai and his fellow courtiers.

At the gate, Mordecai learns of the conspiracy of two eunuchs who were guardians of the threshold. Since the eunuchs had direct access to the royal apartment, they were particularly in a position to slay the monarch. The eunuch Bagoas poisoned Artaxerxes Ochus (338), had his successor Arses assassinated (336), tried to poison Darius III (336), and was compelled by the latter to drink poison himself. On the other hand, the plot of Darius to kill his father, Artaxerxes Memnon, in his bed chamber was betrayed by a eunuch. The framework of the Egyptian collection of wise sayings by Onchscheshonqy is the story of a plot against the life of the Pharaoh. A conspirator speaks of the plot to Onchscheshonqy and a guard overhears the conversation. The plotters are thrown into a flaming furnace and Onchscheshonqy is put into prison.[4] In the Esther story Mordecai denounced the plot, the eunuchs were hanged, but nothing was done for Mordecai, although the Persian kings set great store on rewarding their benefactors. It seems that in Mordecai's tale the delay was explained by the selection of virgins for the royal harem, which happened at this time. The compiler of Esther preserves the rudimentary motif but since he has already narrated the gathering of the girls among whom Esther was chosen (2:3), he now (2:19) speaks of the "second" selection, an expression that puzzles commentators. (The rabbis thought the new bevy of virgins was called to make Esther jealous.) It is a motif which often occurs in Oriental stories and also in Persian history that the monarch in his fondness for the concubines neglects the affairs of state.

As the continuation of the story shows (ch. 6) and as tales of the Arabian Nights illustrate, the right reward for Mordecai would be to promote him to chief minister, but the forgetful king exalts Haman, and all the servants of the king who are in the gate of the king must reverence Haman, whose seat is placed above all the grandees who are with him (3:1). As an ancient Jewish commentator noted, this was an act of ingratitude with regard to Mordecai.[5] Now we understand how the narrator can side with Mordecai against Haman, the royal minister, who has appropriated the rank which rightfully belongs to Mordecai. So Mordecai never bows or pays homage to Haman (3:2). The commentators misunderstand Mordecai's behavior. The Greek translator makes Mordecai say (in an insertion in ch. 4) that he is unwilling to make the worshipful gesture to any but God. Mordecai here refuses to follow the Persian etiquette, which appeared impious to the Greeks. Josephus invents a Jewish law forbidding one to pay obeisance to a mortal man. The rabbis imagined that Haman had an idolatrous image on his robe, or had been a former slave of Mordecai, and so on.

In fact, Mordecai fights for his honor. A man from whom the due reward is withheld by the king protests even if it should cost him his life, as happened to the men who struck down the pretender Cyrus the Younger and dared to say that Artaxerxes II had appropriated the glory of their deed. The Persians kissed their equals on the lips, and kissed the cheek of a person of lower rank. The inferior man meeting a grandee raised the forearm of the right hand and kissed it.[6] The reliefs of Persepolis illustrate this gesture. For Mordecai to pay this respect to Haman would be to "lose face" and acknowledge the new rank of his rival.

The other officials tried to reason with Mordecai but he paid them no heed, though he was transgressing the royal commandment (3:3–4). Then they informed Haman, who in the crowd of flatterers obviously had not noticed Mordecai's behavior. They went to see whether "the words of Mordecai would stand up," that is, as Jerome rightly understood, whether Mordecai would dare to affront the vizir openly. (The compiler of Esther here inserts the notice that Mordecai told them he was a Jew; he needs it to link the two plots, of Mordecai and of Esther.) Haman naturally becomes angry when Mordecai openly defies him (3:5, repeated 5:9). Now he has lost face. He consults his friends (5:14) and decides to hang Mordecai on a gallows fifty cubits high so that everybody can see how he punishes the offender of his honor. The next morning he plans to obtain from the king the condemnation of Mordecai (5:14). But on this night the king cannot sleep and orders the court diaries[7] read to him (6:1). When an Oriental king is sleepless, he wants to be amused. Harun al-Rashid in the Arabian Nights calls a poet or a storyteller to entertain him. From the court journal the king learns how Mordecai has saved his life, and hears from his attendants that nothing has been done for Mordecai. When Haman comes to the royal levee to demand Mordecai's head, he is first asked by the king what should be done to a man whom the king would like to honor. Haman, of course, thinks that the honor is for him and suggests that the royal robe be given to the man to be exalted. This was an exceptional favor. The king now charges Haman to bestow the decoration on Mordecai. This indicated the coming downfall of Haman. As a matter of fact, he ends on the gallows which he has prepared for Mordecai (7:10), just as Nadab is thrown into the dungeon of Achiqar. We do not know how it actually happened. Haman's end was told in the original story of Mordecai. The compiler, combining Esther's and Mordecai's tales, omitted the relevant part of the latter. Did Mordecai tell the king that Haman had been involved in the conspiracy of the eunuchs? The Greek version adds that Haman sought to destroy Mordecai because of the two eunuchs of the king. But it may be only a guess of the translator.

We have here a typical tale of palace intrigue that could as well find a place in the Persian histories of Herodotus and Ctesias, or in the Arabian Nights. The only Jewish element of the tale is that, according to the author, Mordecai is a Jew. The name occurs in Babylonian documents of the Persian period as Mar-duk-a and also appears in the list of the Jews who came back to Jerusalem with Zerubbabel (Ezra 2:2). But the name, which means "man of Marduk" or "worshiper of Marduk," the principal god of Babylon, is not Jewish at all. We may wonder whether the hero of the original tale was a Jew.

~#

Harem Intrigue

The tale of Esther parallels that of Mordecai. This time it is the queen who brings about the downfall of the vizir. The theme is again common in annals and legends of the Oriental courts. Under Khalif al-Mustansir (1036–94) a Jewish leader through influence of the queen mother overthrew a vizir. Roxolana, the famous concubine of Suleiman the Magnificent, made and unmade vizirs. For instance, Ahmed, Suleiman's brother and omnipotent minister, was murdered in the seraglio on March 15, 1536. The chronicles of the court of the Persian kings, as recounted by Ctesias, the Greek physician of Artaxerxes II (405–359), are full of conflicts between royal ministers and the king's wife or mother. These tender females torture, flay, and crucify the favorites of the king, generally eunuchs, who on his order have executed some relatives of the princesses.

In the present text the conflict between the queen and the vizir is accidental. Haman does not know that Esther is Jewish, but his edict against the Jews threatens her life, as Mordecai makes clear (4:13). But this cannot be her motive in the original tale of the conflict. Oriental Jews, followed by the great Moslem savant al-Biruni, knew the habits of Oriental courts and rather imagined that the queen wanted to save her cousin Mordecai from Haman's vengeance. The rabbis, in the same vein, supposed that Haman wanted to marry his daughter to the king, and for this reason they identified him with the councilor who advised the king to repudiate Vashti, his first wife (1:16). But in the book it is not Haman who plots against Esther but she who traps Haman. This is also the theme of the above-mentioned incidents in Persian annals. For instance, the eunuchs of the queen mother Parysatis trick Mithridates, whom she hates, into offending King Artaxerxes II by his boasting, and he is put to death by the king. Likewise, in the Book of Esther, Haman is a thoughtless victim of the queen's cunning. A significant remnant of the original Esther tale seems to have been preserved as a rudimentary motif in 7:8. At the second banquet, during a momentary absence of the king, Haman gets up from his seat to beg Esther for his life. When the king re-enters he sees Haman "fallen upon the couch" of Esther. Since it was a deadly crime even to approach a royal concubine, the rabbis could not understand Haman's gesture. They surmised that the angel Gabriel gave him a push. But by falling upon the couch of Esther, Haman hoped that the queen would protect him with her own body, as Parysatis saved Cyrus the Younger by interposing herself between her guilty son and the royal guards. In the present setting, where Esther is Haman's accuser, the scene makes no sense. An accuser at the Persian court did not waste pity on a fallen foe, for the simple reason that the forgiven enemy would have no forgiveness himself: Cyrus the Younger, pardoned by Artaxerxes II, wanted to avenge his humiliation.

By his foolish act Haman forfeited his life, and was put to death without further ado. Similarly, in 333, Charidemus, a Greek in Persian service, was suspected by the king's friends of conspiring with Alexander. He offended Darius III by his words. The king touched his belt, and Charidemus was dragged off; his throat was cut while he was still appealing to the king. (That Haman was hanged on the gallows made for Mordecai comes from the story of Mordecai.)

In the Bible, Esther, chosen among the virgins brought into the seraglio, becomes queen. Kings' concubines were selected from among "all the women of Asia," as they still were for Alexander centuries later. But the queen came from the royal family or one of the seven princely houses. In the original tale Esther was only a concubine. For thirty days she did not have the honor of the royal couch (4:11)—the women of the harem were sent to the king in regular turns—and she could not come to the king except on his summons. Nobody but the heads of the seven princely houses and the king's wife and mother (as Persian court stories show) was allowed to approach the king without invitation. Eunuchs barred the entry to the men's apartments in the palace. To obtain an audience, it was necessary to approach the chief of the royal guard who was also the head of the administration, or to be favored by an influential eunuch. Esther could not make her request to Haman, nor would a eunuch risk his life, or at least his position, by bringing an unwanted concubine to the king. For the Persian king regarded everybody, except his wife, as a slave.[8]

In the harem Esther kept hidden the secret of her kinship and her people. This could be done and was done. For instance, the future mother of Harun al-Rashid presented herself as an orphan and did not inform the khalif about her family until after the birth of her two sons.[9] In the present setting, there was no reason for Esther to keep the secret. If in the original tale she was the daughter or sister of some rebel put to death by the vizir, her discretion and her hate for Haman would be natural. But here we leave the field of conjectures to enter the fairyland of guesses.

The Story of Vashti

To make the rather trite story of the conflict between the harem and the chancellery more exciting, the
author of the Esther tale prefaced it with the story of
Vashti. The king makes a feast for his people. The Assyrian king Ashurbanipal celebrated the completion of
his royal residence by a banquet for 69,574 guests, as
he himself relates; and Ctesias mentions a banquet for
15,000 guests given by Artaxerxes II. On the seventh day,
"when the heart of the king was merry with wine"
(1:10), he ordered Vashti the queen to be brought, to
show the people and the grandees her beauty. It is the
Candaulus theme, as Voltaire and Gibbon noted, and as
the rabbis believed, saying that Vashti was to appear
naked. King Candaulus of Lydia praised the beauty of
his wife to everybody, and to prove that she was the
fairest of all, without her knowledge gave a friend of
his an opportunity to view her naked. He lost her and
his life. According to the rabbis, Vashti told the king:
"If I come before the lords of the kingdom they will
kill you and marry me." By custom, the wedded wives
could be present at Persian dinners (Neh. 2:6). But they
left when the drinking bout was to begin.[10] At this time,
concubines and courtesans came in. At Belshazzar's feast
(Dan. 5:2) only harem women and concubines are present. The queen comes into the banquet hall only when
Belshazzar is endangered by the writing on the wall
(Dan. 5:10).

By coming to the king's party, Vashti would lose face, she would degrade herself to the position of a concubine. But her refusal poses a grave legal question. In the Persian view, the king is the Law himself. This was the answer of the royal judges when Cambyses wanted to marry his sister.[11] Was Vashti to be allowed to violate the "law" (1:15)? Thus the Candaulus theme passes into another folklore theme: the test of a wife's obedience to her lord. The legal advisers tell the king that Vashti, if pardoned, would make all women flout the orders of their husbands—again the motive is that of losing face. The king accordingly degrades Vashti to the status of a concubine—"she may not come before the king" (1:19)—and explains his decision in a manifesto that reminds women to honor their lords.

The Contamination of the Two Plots

Whatever was the origin of the two tales we have tried to reconstruct, in Jewish folklore the hero and the heroine naturally became Jewish. Later, Jewish readers of the Esther book were embarrassed by the behavior of this Jewish queen who obviously disregards the ritual food laws and does not feel out of place in the harem of a heathen. Lysimachus, the author of the Greek Esther, as early as c. 80 B.C.E. makes Esther say that she abhors the bed of the uncircumcised, does not partake of the food offered, and has had no joy since the day of the change of her destiny. The rabbis assured themselves[12] that in the embrace of Ahasuerus, Esther remained inert like a clod. Christian theologians spoke in this vein of the attitude of the Holy Virgin during the conception of the Savior.[13] The Persian Jews, proud to imagine that one of their kin became chosen by their absolute Lord and Master from among all the virgins of the empire, did not pay attention to these ritual reservations. Nor did the pious Jews of Poland condemn Esterka, the mistress of King Casimir III (1333–70).

Having heard two parallel tales about a Jewish courtier and a Jewish queen who struggled with and overthrew the evil minister of their sovereign, the author of the Book of Esther thought that the stories represented two complementary versions of the same events and accordingly combined them. This was the standard method of ancient writers, who, believing that there is only one truth and that it is attainable, equated and confounded various reports of some historical happening. The rabbis compared the stories of Joseph and Esther. The biblical history of Joseph is also composed of two strains: Joseph is sold by his brethren to the Ishmaelites, yet he is drawn out of the pit by the Midianites who sell him to the Ishmaelites, and so on.

In Jewish folklore, Mordecai the Jewish courtier somehow figured as the savior of the Jews of Susa from some plot of Haman. As we have mentioned, the 14th Adar was sometimes called "the day of Mordecai." The author of the Book of Esther rearranged both popular tales so that his work could become the authoritative explanation of the feast of Purim. He succeeded in this task.

Esther is now the adopted daughter of her uncle Mordecai, and she always takes his advice (2:20). Through his wisdom (2:15) and her own good judgment, she obtains the favor of the head eunuch, pleases the king, and is made queen in the place of Vashti (2:17). Here the author introduces the conflict between Haman and Mordecai.

Haman

Modern commentators anachronistically misinterpret Haman. A German theologian who in Hitler's time had the courage to defend the Book of Esther said that it set the Jewish problem with absolute precision.[14] But there is no "Jewish problem" in the Scroll of Esther. Dante understood the book better. On the terrace of anger in Purgatory he sees victims of blind fury. Procne punished her husband, who had outraged her sister, by killing her own son and serving him as a meal to his father; Amata killed herself because her daughter had been married against her plans. Between them was the crucified Haman, and beside his gallows were Ahasuerus, Esther, and the just Mordecai who was of perfect rectitude in word and deed. In our organized society, we rarely encounter fits of rage and "seeing red." But ancient philosophers wrote extensively on anger, and Dante knew well that proud wrath avenges an insult. Darius I suspected his friend Intaphernes of conspiring against him. He put him and all his kin to death. Haman wanted to kill Mordecai and his whole tribe "the people of Mordecai" (3:6), be they Jews or, say, Kurds, to wash out in a sea of blood the stain of a public insult.

Ahasuerus, the Shah, is like a modern general who gives routine approval to the reasoned opinion of his chief of staff. Haman argues as follows (3:8): "There is a certain unimportant people,[15] scattered and separated among the peoples of the realm. Their laws differ from the laws of all other peoples." The inference is that the king may proceed against this people without endangering the general peace of the empire. Secondly: "The laws of the king they do not observe." This marks them as subversive. Darius I and Xerxes again and again, and in identical words, stress the "law" or "laws" of the king as keeping the multinational empire together. This law should be feared so that the strong do not destroy the weak. Enumerating his provinces, the Great King adds that by favor of the supreme god Ahuramazda these countries show respect toward his law.[16]

In both his arguments, Haman implies that "it is not suitable for the king to let them rest [as they are now]." There may be various solutions to the governmental problem posed by the sagacious vizir. For instance, Persian kings often transplanted unruly subjects into some other province. But since the people in question are already scattered, this measure would not help. So Haman proposes to destroy them, and he offers to pay 10,000 talents of silver to the royal treasury. As Josephus noted, this is the head price for the people who might have been sold as slaves for the profit of the king.

Haman's Edict

According to the Babylonian view accepted in the whole Near East, at the beginning of each year the gods predetermined men's destinies. When the sixth day came, "lucky lots" were distributed by Heaven among the earth's inhabitants. For this reason the Persians called this day "the day of hope." [17]

The author of the Book of Esther believed, and rightly, that the word "Purim" means "lots" (3:7). He therefore supposed that Haman, insulted by Mordecai, awaited the next New Year's festival period (probably Nisan 6th) to cast lots before him to find out the favorable day for his vengeance. Afterwards, he went to the king to obtain the royal consent to his decree, and sent copies of the order into all the king's provinces on the thirteenth of the first month (3:12).

Purim, however, was celebrated in Adar, the twelfth month, and thus the author of the Book of Esther had to place the date of the massacre eleven months after the issuance of Haman's decree. This delay did not trouble the author or his readers. The synchronization of administrative actions demanded time in the conditions of ancient technology. In 88 B.C.E. Mithridates VI of Pontus ordered a general slaughter of "all who were of Italic race," men, women, and children of every age, in the Roman province of Asia which he had just conquered. The killing was to be done at the same time everywhere, namely on the thirtieth day after the date of the royal order. The Roman province of Asia covered the western part of Asia Minor. Ahasuerus, however, reigned over one hundred and twenty-seven provinces from India to Ethiopia (1:1). Haman needed much more time than Mithridates to bring about the simultaneous massacre on the given day in all these provinces. An order of Antiochus III, issued in February, 193 B.C.E., was forwarded by his viceroy in Iran on June 25th.[18]

Mithridates' orders to satraps and cities were sealed.

The construction of the plot in the Book of Esther demands that Haman's orders be made public immediately. Thus, from Voltaire on,[19] modern authors wonder why the Jews did not use the months between Nisan and Adar for attacking their enemies or simply for flight.

Yet the author of Esther like a Puck complicates the problem: Mordecai's counteracting edict is issued on the 23d day of the third month (8:9). If Haman terrified the Jews for some seventy days, Mordecai keeps both the Jews and their enemies in suspense for almost nine months. The problem of delay was solved by Bossuet. In his fifth "Avertissement" to the Protestants (1690) he contrasts the conduct of the Jews with the later plots against Louis XIV. The Jews, even in danger of extermination, did not undertake anything against their lawful sovereign. In the Persian view, the king ruled by the will of the Creator. As Xerxes said, "Ahuramazda gave us the earth, the sky, the mankind, and he also made Xerxes rule the multitude." Darius said that the subject countries were given him by Ahuramazda. "What was said unto them by me either by night or by day, was done."

In the political theology of the Persian kings, their will was identical with truth and righteousness, the attributes of the Supreme God. A rebel was also faithless, and his insubordination a "lie." [20] Thus, to quote Bossuet again (*Histoire universelle*), the Jews could only hope that, touched by their tears, God would change the heart of Ahasuerus.

Esther became the instrument of salvation. The rabbis made Ahasuerus reproach the queen for having concealed her origin. Had he known it, he would not have given the order for destruction. But in Esther's Scroll the king does not even know the name of the people to be destroyed. He does not even seal (that is, ratify) the decree. Trusting in his minister, he gives him his signet ring (3:10). But Haman does not know that the queen is Jewish and thus he falls into her trap.

It is unnecessary to dwell on the decision of Esther to come to the king uninvited, to tell again how her charms conquered Ahasuerus—various painters (Tintoretto, Veronese, Rubens, Poussin, Claude Lorrain) and Racine understood the magical effects of the scene—nor to repeat what has been said about the fate of Haman. Mordecai succeeded him as vizir, and the tables were turned in favor of the Jews.

Mordecai's Decree

After the fall of Haman, Esther asked Ahasuerus to annul Haman's decree, but the king answered that the royal order signed with the king's ring is irrevocable (8:8). The idea that the royal word is unalterable comes from theology. Of Oriental gods it is said again and again that their decision is unalterable. A capricious and fickle omnipotence would be insufferable. "A human king," say the rabbis, "may choose whether or not to obey his own decree. But if God issues a decree, He is the first to obey it." [21]

In this respect, the Oriental kings imitated the gods.[22] It means not that every utterance of the king was unchangeable but that "the statutes of Persia and Media," could not be changed. In expressing this idea, the authors of Daniel (6:9, 6:13) and of Esther (1:19) use the Persian loan-word *dat*. To become a statute, the order must be in writing and the writing ratified by inscription of the royal name by means of the royal seal, as we learn from Daniel 6:9–11 and Esther 8:8. According to Esther 1:19, the decree, to become irrevocable, must also be entered "into the statutes of Persia and Media." In the present state of our ignorance of Persian institutions we are unable to check the exactness of these data.

Unable to cancel Haman's decree, the new vizir must circumvent it. Thus, to understand Mordecai's edict we have first to realize the legal effects of Haman's edict. Haman does not mobilize royal forces against the Jews. The central government and its satraps would be unable to cope with the task of organizing and carrying out a massacre on the whole territory of the immense empire. But Haman's edict, published in all the provinces, marks the Jews as outlaws. The protection of the king is withdrawn from them. They may be killed and deprived of property by anybody with impunity. Mithridates outlawed the Romans in the same way, but added that the bodies of the victims should remain unburied.

An outlaw became a common enemy. It was fitting to cleanse the land from his contamination. When Antiochus III executed his vizir Hermias, the latter's wife was killed by women and her sons by boys of the city of Apamea. Therefore, Haman calls on "all peoples" in Ahasuerus' empire to slay the Jews. Likewise, the Greek cities of Asia and city mobs carried out the massacre of Romans as ordered by Mithridates. Both Haman and Mithridates addressed their letters not only to the royal governors but also to the local authorities: "to the lords of every people" (3:12). Likewise the massacre on the day of St. Bartholomew (Aug. 24, 1572), though plotted by the court and approved by Charles IX, was organized by the magistrates of Paris on his order.

Mordecai's edict grants the right of self-defense to

the outlawed Jews. They may gather and "stand for their life." They may (with impunity) kill those who would "harass" them, their wives and children, and plunder their goods. The edict describes these would-be enemies as "all armed forces of people and provinces" (8:11) and the letters were prepared to every province in its script and to every people (translated) in its language (8:9; cf. 1:22; 3:12).[23] We may again note the massacre of the Romans in the Greek cities of Asia and the day of St. Bartholomew, on which the "provost of merchants," sheriffs, and aldermen of Paris assembled and armed the citizenry to kill the Huguenots.[24] Following the edict of Mordecai the Jews "laid hands upon such as sought to harm them" (9:2). Their enemies also attacked (9:16), but were defeated, and the Jews could "avenge themselves upon their enemies."

The royal government remained neutral. No mention is made of royal forces called to destroy or to protect the Jews, although in the end, because of Mordecai, the provincial governors helped the Jews (9:3) as they would have aided their enemies if Haman had still been at the helm of the empire. (In III Maccabees, a book written in the highly centralized Egypt of the Ptolemies, the Jews are rounded up by royal forces and are to be massacred by royal elephants.)

The neutrality of the king amid a civil war in his empire may seem to us absurd. To the ancient Persians who boasted that anyone could travel unmolested through the empire it would seem absurd that the omnipotent governments of today remain neutral in labor conflicts which close all ports of the country.

Ancient empires were far from being omnipotent. They were, indeed, weak superstructures. Man's first loyalty was to his tribe or his city, and feuds between cities and tribes were endemic. Describing the army of

Vespasian marching against Jerusalem, Tacitus mentions "the band of Arabs hostile to the Jews whom they hate as is usual between neighbors." Tacitus was a Roman senator living in the age when the emperors maintained with difficulty the *pax romana* on the whole earth from London to Baghdad. The Persian kings did not and could not have the same ambition. They intervened in petty wars of subject peoples haphazardly and for opportunist reasons. Letters of Artaxerxes II compelled his satrap Datames to raise the siege of Sinope. The same king listened to the appeal of three cities of Cyprus threatened by the ambitions of Euagoras of Salamis after the latter had reduced other cities of Cyprus. Under Artaxerxes I, Nehemiah, the royal governor of Judea, begins to rebuild the walls of Jerusalem. The neighboring Samaritans led by the royal governor Sanballat, the Arabs, the Ammonites on the other side of the Jordan, and the city of Ashdod on the Mediterranean coast form a coalition "to come and fight against Jerusalem . . . slay them and make the work cease" (Neh. 4). Nehemiah mobilizes the people and comforts the Jews by appealing to God's awful might. He does not appeal to Artaxerxes II.

Mordecai's edict established parity between the Jews and their enemies. In the ensuing war, the Jews won. Who were these enemies? The author does not say and does not need to say. In a society where every tribe remained a separate unit but where at the same time men of various tribes lived in the same localities and rubbed shoulders with one another, frictions were inevitable. The Jews, like any group, had their enemies, and Haman's edict would naturally swell their number and lead to an explosion of greed and hate: blood and booty are powerful means of recruitment. In turn the Jews hate and kill their enemies. The author tells about it with the detachment of a reporter and the satisfaction of a man of folk wisdom: "Who digs a pit shall fall therein" (Prov. 26:27). A famous German nursery tale describes with pleasure how Gretel threw the witch into her own oven.

But the Book of Esther breathes no hate against the Gentiles. On the contrary, the author goes out of his way to isolate Haman, to show that his decree was an act of personal vengeance. Even his wife and his advisers warn him (6:13). The king was deceived by Haman: it is significant that Haman does not name the people he wants to slay in his report to the king. When Haman's edict was published, the city of Susa was grieved (3:15), and the same city rejoiced at Mordecai's appointment (8:15).

Haman, the New Amalek

Yet the story has a second plan. As Josephus understood, Haman and Mordecai followed the law of vendetta. Haman was an Agagite, a descendant of the king Agag of the Amalekites, who had been captured by Saul and slain on the insistence of Samuel. He is of the race of which the Torah says: "The Lord will have war with Amalek from generation to generation" (Exod. 17:16), and again "You shall blot out the remembrance of Amalek from under heaven" (Deut. 25:19). Mordecai is a descendant of Saul. The personal conflict of two courtiers is also a part of the providential plan. As Rabbi Levi, a Palestinian of the fourth century, explained, had Saul not spared Amalek there would have been no Haman.[25]

The author did not need to labor the point. The

mention of Kish, Saul's father (I Sam. 9:1), at the end of Mordecai's geneology (2:5) and the statement that Haman was an Agagite (3:1) oriented the readers. They understood that while the decrees of both Haman and Mordecai allowed each side to take the spoils of the adversary, and that while Haman counted on the booty (3:13)—"We are sold," cries Esther to the king (7:4)—the Jews did not plunder their victims (9:10). They were not selfless, but remembered that the Amalekites, the most ancient foes of Israel, should be utterly destroyed (I Sam. 15:21) with their spoils. On this second level, we may say by hindsight that the issue of the conflict is foreordained. The reader knows in advance that Amalek cannot destroy Israel.

Readers may well wonder why in a book in which the Persian king and kingship are mentioned some 250 times, God is never mentioned; why, except for the fast appointed by Esther before her going to the king (4:16), no religious action is referred to. The Greek translator accordingly interpolated long prayers and other religious trappings. But for the author of Esther, the merit of salvation belongs not to Esther, or Mordecai, or the Jews of Susa, or to their tears and supplications, but to God alone who pursues His plan independent of human wishes or fears. He saves the Jews of Susa and of the Persian Empire not for their sake but because their would-be slayer is a cursed Agagite. Matthew Henry, nonconformist New England divine, wrote in his *Exposition of the Old and the New Testament* (1704): "Though the name of God is not in it, the finger of God is, directing many minute events for the bringing about of His people's deliverance." And he quotes the Psalm (37:12): "The wicked plots against the righteous, and gnashes his teeth at him; but the Lord laughs at the wicked, for He sees that his day is coming."

Israel should never forget that Amalek had attacked the faint and weak at the rear of Israel's train marching in the wilderness (Deut. 25:18). But that does not mean that God knew that from Agag would rise an adversary of the Jews, as the rabbis said with reference to Haman.[26] This resuscitation in contemporary history of the primeval history of a nation is foreign to the mentality of the ancient Near East. As late as the fourth century, for the Chronicler (I Chron. 4:42) the destruction of the rest of the Amalekites in the time of King Hezekiah had no symbolic meaning.

The recurrent influence of motifs of the hoary past is rather a Greek peculiarity. In 480 the Cretans ask the Delphic Oracle whether they should take part in the Persian war. Apollo replies that they are fools. Though the Greeks had not paid for the death of the Cretan king Minos in Sicily, the Cretans fought in the Trojan war to exact retribution for the rape of Helen, and then were punished by famine and pestilence. Euripides is said to have been bribed by the Corinthians to make Medea (and not the Corinthians) kill her sons in his tragedy. Agathocles of Syracuse replied to the Corcyrans that he devastated their land because their forebears had received Odysseus who had blinded the Sicilian Polyphemus.[27] After the destruction of Jerusalem in 70 c.e. the rabbis, in the Greek manner, identify Rome with Amalek and Esau, who was Amalek's grandfather (Gen. 36:12).

In their view, the deliverance of the Jews of Susa and Persia from a new Amalek became a part of the universal pattern of history. Purim should be kept yearly by all the Jews and by all who should join themselves to them everywhere and forever (9:27). Though the Book of Esther is the only one in the Bible and among the Apocrypha that contains no reference to the Holy Land, it was translated into Greek in Maccabean Jerusalem to make it accessible to the whole Diaspora. In 78/77 this "Epistle of Phurim" (cf. 9:30) was brought to the Jews of Alexandria and registered there. The Synagogue reads the condemnation of Amalek (Deut. 25:17) on the Sabbath which precedes Purim.

Purim

Yet the Book of Esther is not a *Te Deum* of triumph, and Purim does not commemorate a victory, or even a deliverance. The Greeks often established a commerative feast. For instance, the city of Oxyrhynchus in Egypt, two centuries after the event, continued to celebrate a victory over the Jews during the great Jewish rebellion of 117 C.E. In the same Greek style, after the victory over Nicanor, a general of Demetrius I of Syria, the Jews of Jerusalem in 160 B.C.E. founded an annual commemoration of their success. But Purim is celebrated by feasting and gladness and sending dainties to one another on the day which follows the battle. It is a day of feasting which became a "day of pleasure" (9:19).[28] This is strange. The Passover is celebrated on the day on which Israel came out of Egypt (Exod. 13:3) and not the next day. But the author of the Book of Esther did not understand the feast whose origins he wanted to explain.

The explanation may lie elsewhere. Young men form bands which fight one another just for the sheer pleasure of fighting and of breaking routine. In our organized society this universal phenomenon of immature power is treated as juvenile delinquency. The pre-industrial world channelized much of youthful passion by making its expressions, such as the fist fights between two groups, a part of some general festival. The theologians hallowed the same phenomenon by giving it a magical significance. In Babylon a battle was conceived as taking place annually between Tiamat, the force of Chaos, and Marduk, the divine patron of Babylon, at the New Year festival in Spring.[29] Hittite texts of the second millennium B.C.E. describe the Autumn festival of the god Yarris at which the young men were divided into two bands, "men of Hatti" and "men of Masa," which fought each other. Of course, the "men of Hatti" won and devoted a captive to the god. Such sham fights are often referred to in classical and medieval sources and were common in Europe until our century.[30]

Modern scholars taking the ritualist trappings for the real thing imagine that these mock conflicts were seasonal rites originally representing the victory of Summer over Winter, and so on. Ancient scholars preferred a historical interpretation. For instance, the Persians celebrated an uproarious—"bacchic," as the Greeks said—festival of *Sacaea*. Greek (or native) savants concluded from its name that this festival commemorated the victory over the Sacae, a Scythian people. According to one version, heard at Zela in Pontus, the Sacae on one of their raids plundered Zela, got drunk, and were killed to the last man by Persian generals, who then established the festival in honor of the goddess Anahita. According to another version, the Sacae celebrated a victory and on this occasion were cut to pieces by Cyrus. Another Persian festival, celebrated at Susa, was explained as the commemoration of "the slaughtering of the Magi" after the overthrow of a Magus who, passing himself off as Smerdis, brother and successor of King Cambyses, for two years occupied the throne (522–520). On that festival day no Magus dared to appear in the streets. In a later interpretation, Alexander was charged with murdering the Magi.[31] As a matter of fact, the whole story of Pseudo-Smerdis seems to have been a propaganda trick of Darius I, who killed the successor Cambyses. According to Darius, this happened in Media. But the local tradition, repeated by Herodotus, placed the death of the Magus at Susa, to give a quasi-historical explanation of a seasonal festival. Ritual combats between two halves of the same tribe or two parts of the same town were common in Iran. In Moslem times such combats developed into fights between Shiites and Sunnites, between different Sunnite movements, between different sects, and so on. For instance, the anniversary of the death of the hated Khalif Omar (634–644) was yearly celebrated in Persia. The populace cursed Omar and at times an Armenian was hired to impersonate him.[32]

In Susa, the Jews were numerous and rich and proud of their city, the ancient capital of Persian kings. A relief on a gate of the Herodian Temple in Jerusalem represented the city of Susa.[33] Their seasonal mock fight was performed for two days, the 13th and the 14th Adar, that is in the early Spring, just a month before Passover. In the surrounding villages the Jews, less rich and less numerous, had the same performance on one day only: the 13th Adar. The bands were called "the Jews" and the anonymous "enemies" and, of course, "our side" triumphed. This was a good omen, and in the evening, that is, according to the lunar reckoning on the next calendar day, the Jews happily rested and enjoyed the "day of pleasure." The Jews of Susa also told stories about a beautiful Persian queen of Jewish race who overthrew a vile vizir and about a wise Mordecai, who likewise cast from power an evil vizir, became minister himself, and, of course, "sought the good of his people, and worked for the welfare of all his kindred" (10:3).

The Purim Tale

A Jew from Susa, writing probably in the second century B.C.E. (see p. 187), combined the two popular stories and used them to explain the Purim feast of Susa and its countryside. The operation produced some duplications which perplex modern scholars. They ask, for instance, why, after the execution of Haman and the elevation of Mordecai, did Esther need to supplicate the king to counteract Haman's massacre order (8:3–7)? But it was Esther who in the folk tale had saved her kin. The author of the Scroll, a master of literary craft, knew how to add the charm of variety to his parallel accounts. As the Greek version and rabbinical commentaries show, ancient readers did notice repetitions and contradictions in the Scroll. Its author had two heroes and had to explain two different dates of Purim: the 14th Adar in villages (9:19) and the 15th Adar at Susa. He made Mordecai take care of the provincial Jews (9:2–5) and, as in the original Mordecai's tale, execute Haman's sons (9:7). This involved the destruction of the enemies in "the fortress of Susa" (9:6), that is, the royal residence, and explained the mock fights of the 13th Adar in Susa and the countryside. But in Susa, the ritual battle continued on the 14th Adar. This gave the author the occasion to assign a role to Esther: she obtains from the king the permission to continue the fight on the 14th Adar in order to clean up the city (not the fortress) of Susa, and to hang Haman's sons (9:12–14). (The catastrophe of the hateful vizir in the Esther tale naturally involved his kin.) In this way the author adroitly separates the parallel actions of Esther and Mordecai in time and space.

Chronological discrepancies are more disconcerting. Esther's marriage falls in the seventh year of Artaxerxes (2:16), but Haman's decree was issued in the beginning of the twelfth year of the same king (3:7). This five-year gap is unexplained and is unnecessary in the present narrative. The author, professing to write history, probably found both dates in his sources.

As we have mentioned, Purim was originally a feast of the Jews at Susa and its countryside. The country Jews who dwelt in unwalled places celebrated Purim on the 14th Adar (9:19) whereas the Jews of Susa kept it on the 15th (9:18). But the author of the Scroll wants to make this local feast recognized by all Jews. Accordingly, he makes Haman and Mordecai issue a general order and a counterorder concerning all "the 127 provinces" of the realm, and speaks generally of the "cities" in these provinces (9:2), and again summarizes this universal danger for the Jews (9:2–5) to explain the institution of Purim on the 14th Adar (9:5). Again, having two heroes, he can twice develop his ecumenical appeal. First Mordecai sends the message to the Jews in all the provinces of the realm to keep the 14th and the 15th Adar (here the author generalizes the ritual difference between the Jews of the City of Susa and the dwellers in its countryside. Then Esther and Mordecai write again to "confirm" the celebration of Purim on the appointed days. It was "the commandment of Esther" which gave the statutory quality to the festival. For this reason her letter was recorded in "the roll" (cf. Ezra 6:2), that is, the register of royal acts (9:31–32).

It is remarkable that the orders coming from Susa are supplemented by the resolutions of the local Jewish communities. The Jews "impose on themselves and accept" what Mordecai has written to them (9:23, 27), and they are called to "institute" the celebration of Purim as they had ordained "for themselves and their seed" fastings in bygone times (9:31).[34] Thus, at least theoretically, they could also refuse to accept the festival, but they agreed "not to transgress" this obligation forever (9:27). We are no longer in the Persian Empire but in the Hellenistic Age. Each community of the Diaspora is an independent unit. In the same manner, according to III Maccabees, the Jews of Egypt, delivered from a great peril, decide to celebrate the anniversary of the event. The supposititious letter of Judah Maccabaeus to the Jews of Egypt at the beginning of II Maccabees offers a parallel to the Purim Scroll. Judah allegedly going to establish Hanukkah tells relevant events, and suggests to the Jews of Egypt that they will do well if they also keep this festival. Again, the apocryphal Book of Baruch (in the Greek and Latin Bibles) was allegedly sent by the Jews of Babylonia to the Jews of Jerusalem to be read in the Temple.

Greek cities and devotees, in the same way, made propaganda for their respective gods and published records attesting their power. But in idolatrous worship, a man, say the Egyptian priest Apollonius, could bring "his god with him" at Delos. A transmission of a new festival meant the introduction of a new cult. The cities rather preferred to become places of pilgrimage to their shrines. The God of the Jews was omnipresent, although His sacrificial worship had to be performed in Jerusalem. Thus, a new Jewish festival could be accepted in other

Jewish communities. In the same way many Christian feasts, for instance those in honor of the Blessed Virgin, started as local celebrations, were imitated elsewhere, and then became ecumenical. The Jews of Susa and of Persia gladly accepted the scroll that flattered them and perfectly agreed with the historical sight of the age. For instance, the Greek inhabitants of Lampsacus narrated that the first settlers had learned from the daughter of the king of their barbarian neighbors that the latter planned to attack and slay them because of envy and fear. Under the pretext of sacrifice, they made the plotters come into the *faubourg* of the city, destroyed them, named their city after the benefactress, and lived happily ever after.

The triumph of the Hasmoneans made the Book of Esther particularly welcome to the Dispersion. They too could now boast of divine intervention on their behalf. They read in the book that after the appointment of Mordecai, "many of the peoples of the earth" (Deut. 28:10) "gave themselves out as Jews, for the fear of the Jews had fallen upon them" (8:17). The promise given to the Chosen People in the Holy Land (Exod. 23:27) was also fulfilled in the Diaspora: if you will obey God's commandments, God will lay the fear of you upon the nations (Deut. 11:25).

A Hebrew-reading Jew of Greek culture found everything he could desire in the Book of Esther. Here the people whom God saved were no longer the uncouth patriarchs and the wild prophets but men of polite society who could have held office at the Hellenistic court. The king who, as a rabbi later said, sacrificed his (first) wife to a friend and then his friend to his (second) wife, who could promise to grant any request (5:3), and who would refuse money offered him (3:11) looked like a double of a Seleucid, a Ptolemy, or a Parthian ruler. The reader was happy to find in a Hebrew book motifs fa-

miliar from the Greek school. Mordecai advising Esther
to go to Ahasuerus was like Otanes in Herodotus instruct-
ing his daughter Phaedyme, a concubine of Pseudo-
Smerdis, to learn the latter's true identity. Like Esther,
Phaedyme hesitates to risk her life; like Esther, she obeys
her outside master; like Esther she wins.[35]

The Esther Scroll also offered the attraction of local
color, a feature much in demand by Hellenistic readers,
who enjoyed historical novels about bygone royalty, be
it Ninus of Assyria or Esther of Persia. Touches stressing
the Persian background of the story also impress the
modern reader of Esther. As a matter of fact, most of
these details are rather permanent features of Oriental
despotism. The shahs seen by J. B. Chardin (1643–1713)
during his stays in Persia are like Ahasuerus. The reader
of his voyages feels the atmosphere of the Book of Esther.
A French missionary of the eighteenth century could
offer a very instructive "parallel between Chinese man-
ners and the Book of Esther." [36]

Some court ceremonies remained essentially the same
over millennia. Giving royal garments as a reward (6:8)
was practiced by the Macedonian rulers of Persia as well
as by the shahs in the seventeenth century. Genesis
(41:43), Esther (6:11), I Maccabees (10:62), and the
traveler Chardin all describe how the man honored by
the king was led through the city by royal officers proclaiming his merits. Receiving the royal signet (3:10;
8:2), marked the elevation to viceregal authority in the
days of the Pharaohs (Gen. 41:42) as well as in the age
of Alexander and his successors.

As a matter of fact, the author's knowledge of the
Persian court is not precise enough. The king set Haman's
seat "above all the lords who were with him" (3:1). Thus,
Haman appears as a great vizir, the foremost man of a
collegiate government similar to or identical with the

council of seven in Esther 1:14. As a matter of fact, the man "next to the king" (10:3) was the commander of the bodyguard and for this reason functioned as his representative and his chief officer. This "chiliarch," as the Greeks translated the Persian title, held "the second rank in power," as a Latin author says. The chiliarch was "the most trusted man," as Herodotus tells us.[37] The military position of Haman probably explains why Esther invited him twice and attacked him only at the second banquet (7:1). She had first to lull Haman's suspicions. Otherwise, the commander of the pretorians might be able to get rid of her and of the king himself. Xerxes, called Ahasuerus in the Bible (cf. Ezra 4:6) was assassinated in 465 by the commander of his guard. But the author of Esther's Scroll did not understand the hints in his source. He lived in the Hellenistic age and his Seleucid king had a sort of Secretary of State for all departments.

The author wrote before 78/77 B.C.E., the date at which the Greek version of his Scroll was brought to Alexandria.[38] Thus, he must have lived in the second or third century B.C.E. But if his exact date as yet remains uncertain, there can be no doubt as to the place of his activity. A man who wrote to make a festival of Susa ecumenical was a man of this city. Several Greek authors of the same age tried to render the same service to their respective cities. For instance, a decree of Chersonesus, in the Crimea, praises the local historian Syriscus for having reported the wondrous deeds of the city goddess.[39]

The topographic references in the Scroll of Esther are rather general. Every palace would have gates (2:19; 4:6; 5:9), inner and outer courts (4:11; 5:1; 6:4), and gardens (7:7). The "broad place of the town" before the palace gate (4:6; 5:9), again, has no definition. Unfortunately, the palace area was excavated at a time when archaeological method was as yet unknown. Today the visitor at Susa finds only deep pits burrowed by the excavators in the flank of the mounds. But the author of Esther exactly and rightly distinguishes between *Shushan ha birah*, "the fortress of Susa" (2:5; 9:11. Cf. 1:2; 3:15; 8:14), where the palace stood, and *ha ir Shushan*, "the town of Susa" (3:15; 8:15), which lay at the foot (eastward) of the acropolis. Modern commentators imagine that the author here committed an error. They are misled by the terminology of the French excavators, who called the southern mound "acropolis" and the northern mound "palace." In fact, the "fortress of Susa" probably embraced both hills. In any case, Nehemiah tells us (Neh. 1:1) that he, just like Mordecai after him (2:5), lived in "the fortress of Susa."

As a man of Susa, the author of Esther could easily find picturesque traits such as the twelve months of cosmetic preparation for every new concubine of the king (2:12) in the folklore of the ancient capital of the Achaemenids, where the palace built by Darius still dominated the city.[40]

Southeast of Susa the semi-independent rulers of Elymais (Elam) continued the Achaemenid tradition. Farther southeast, some twenty days of caravan travel from Susa, in the heart of Persia proper, at Pasargadae there was another semi-independent Persian court. As the coin legends of these principalities show, their official language was Aramaic, that is, the mother tongue of the Eastern Jews in the Hellenistic age, the language currently spoken also in Susa. (In a Greek hymn written at Susa, Apollo is called *mara*, that is, "Lord" in Aramaic.) Vocabulary and syntax of the Book of Esther betray Aramaic influence.[41]

Susa obeyed the Macedonian Seleucids until c. 147 B.C.E., when the city came into the hands first of a king of Elymais, then of the Parthians. But even if the author

of Esther wrote before c. 147, he lived in an environment
that was permeated by Iranian traditions. The Persian
administrative terms he uses were loan words in Aramaic
—he does not need to explain them. The thirty-odd
Persian personal names in the book, such as Memucan
(1:16), the Zoroastrian name meaning "good thought,"
he could find by looking around among his Iranian neighbors.[42] But his heroes Mordecai and Esther bear Babylonian names. Mordecai is named after Marduk, the tutelary
deity of Babylon. Esther is Ishtar, the Venus of the Babylonians. The Jews of the Hellenistic age did not scruple
to give this kind of name to their children. Often a Jew
had two names: a Jewish one and a Greek, e.g., Jonathan/
Apollonios. Thus, the author says (2:7), that Esther was
also called Hadassah. Hadassah is generally understood
as "myrtle" but it was probably a Babylonian word meaning "bride." [43]

"Ishtar who dwells in Susa" was worshiped in the
Persian capital, but the main deity of the city was Nanaia,
called Artemis by the Greeks. The author, however,
wanted to stress the Babylonian origin of Mordecai and
Esther. As in the case of Daniel (Dan. 1:13), it was de-
sirable for a Diaspora family to descend from the people
who were carried away with Jehoiakim, king of Judah,
in 597 (Esther 2:6), because this captivity included the
nobility of Jerusalem (II Kings 24:12) while the depor-
tation in 586 concerned the commoners (II Kings 25:11).
As Mordecai and Esther symbolized the Jewry of Susa,
the author indirectly flattered his community.

The Book of Esther had a beautiful heroine and a
royal romance, just like Greek love novels, and like them
contained no unseemly word. Beautifully written, the
Scroll offended no one. Except Haman, there is no evil
man, and, as the great Austrian playwright Grillparzer
(1791–1872) wrote, if Haman represented vainglory

Mordecai represented pride.[44] The success of this "best seller" was such that in Alexandria someone soon invented a parallel story: Ptolemy Physcon (c. 144 B.C.E.) decides to destroy all the Jews of Alexandria but they are saved by the intervention of his favorite, Irene.

The authorities of the Holy Land never granted the status of a holy day to Purim. The *Hallel* (Psalms of Praise, 113–8, recited every morning of the Hanukkah festival) is not recited in the Synagogue on Purim, nor is manual work forbidden on that day. Though the Scroll of Esther was read in the Synagogue before 70 C.E., the recital of the usual benedictions before and after the reading was unknown as late as 200 C.E., and is not mentioned before 400 C.E. In fact, the rabbis objected to Esther's and Mordecai's presumption in establishing a national festival arbitrarily.

But the literary success of Esther's Scroll carried Purim to triumph. It is significant that the Scroll is the only portion of Scripture that may be read in any language in the Synagogue. It is no less indicative that all Purim rules of the rabbis were based on the Scroll.[45] Later, when the dark age came and real Hamans played the role of the fictitious Agagite so efficiently, Purim and Esther and her Scroll became the palladium of the Diaspora. For the Marranos who had to hide their true faith, Esther was the symbol of their own fate. In her *Corinna* (1807) Madame de Staël relates that the Jews of Papal Rome refused to pass under the Arch of Titus, the destroyer of Jerusalem. She adds: "I hope the anecdote is true. It would honor the Jews. Long remembering goes with long sufferings." (*Les longs ressouvenirs conviennent aux longs malheurs.*)

The Appreciation of the Scroll of Esther

Because the estimate of the Book of Esther in this essay is at variance with common opinion, it is fitting to explain the origin of the latter.

It was natural for this story of salvation, which parallels the wonder of the Exodus, to be celebrated by the Jews. Simeon ben Lakish (c. 300) declared that, like the Torah and its Halachic interpretation, the Scroll of Esther would not pass away after the coming of the Messiah, and Maimonides reiterated this view. Probably both felt with Rabbi Assi (c. 300) that, alas, the time of miracles ended with Esther.

The Church, which considered itself the new and true Israel, valued no less the wonderful event that had saved the people of the Lord. Beginning with Clement of Rome (c. 100), ecclesiastical writers glorified the perfect faith of Esther and her beauty which brought about the deliverance of Israel. She was viewed as the prototype of the Church and, later, of the Virgin Mary, though she was not venerated in the East among the saints of the Old Dispensation.[46]

As to Haman, the enemy of the Jews: looking toward the altar wall of the Sistine Chapel in the Vatican, on one side one sees the Brazen Serpent lifted up in the Wilderness, a prototype of the Crucifixion of the Son of Man (John 3:14), and on the other side the crucified Haman. Michelangelo represented him as seen by Dante:

dispettoso e fiero, who even dying is scornful and ferocious. In medieval symbolism the punishment of Haman antitypically prefigured Jesus on the Cross. Mordecai was the figure of Christ, and Haman an embodiment of Satan. Thus, his death, as Rupertus of Deutz (c. 1100) explains, was "the most beautiful image of the future triumph of the Redeemer." [47]

The Book of Esther attracted readers not only for its symbolic meaning, but also as a work of belles-lettres. Athanasius of Alexandria (c. 300–373), though leaving Esther (as well as Ecclesiasticus, the Wisdom of Solomon, etc.) outside the biblical canon, recommends these books as works of edification "for the sake of piety." The tale of Esther became a preferred subject of miracle plays and later of the religious theater, from Spain to Moscow. Lope de Vega (1560–1635) wrote *La hermosa Ester*, and the first play in Russian, produced before Czar Alexis in 1672, was *Artaxerxes' Play*, based on the Book of Esther. G. F. Handel composed his oratorio *Esther* in 1720.

The first to condemn the Book of Esther was Luther. Modern commentators reproduce his judgment without understanding it. In his *Table Talk*, Luther said that he was hostile to II Maccabees and Esther "for they judaize too much and have too much of heathen corruption (*Unart*)." The second reproach is directed against the imagery of the Oriental court and its intrigues. The first one means that Esther cannot be applied to forward the doctrine that the Old Testament foreshadows the life of Jesus. Luther was accordingly indignant that the Jews of his time valued Esther more than Daniel and Isaiah, who, for Luther, predicted the coming of Christ. If we accept the postulate that the New Testament is hidden in the Old Testament and the Old Testament is revealed in the New Testament (Augustine), this view of Luther's is both logical and legitimate.

While denying the Book of Esther its place as a source of Christian faith, Luther nevertheless recognizes its moral value. As he says in the Preface to his German translation of the book, it contains "much that is good." Esther, like Sarah and Judith, is a woman inspired by the Holy Ghost. He names Esther as a model to follow in his work *On the Duties of Christian Spouses.*[48]

Anyway, after Luther, in two centuries of religious wars the Lutherans no less than the Roman Catholics proudly identified themselves with the persecuted Hebrews and regarded the foe as Haman's seed. For instance, after the failure of the Gunpowder Plot (1605) an Anglican divine drew a lengthy and detailed comparison between the time of Esther "and that of the Powder treason." The hostile sects all dreamed of hanging their own Haman and his sons. John Knox, a founder of the Church of Scotland, describing (1546) the murder of Cardinal Beaton, "an obstinate enemy against Christ Jesus," added: "These things we write merrily."

On February 16, 1568, a sentence of the Holy Office, approved by Pope Pius V, condemned the whole population of the Netherlands as heretics and thus liable to the death penalty. Philip II of Spain ordered this sentence carried out without regard to age and sex. The same Saint Pius V, for the sake of the honor of the almighty God, in his letter of March 28, 1569, recommended to the Queen-Regent of France to kill all Protestants in her realm.[49]

On the other hand, the court atmosphere of the Book of Esther made it a convenient vehicle for hidden reference to court intrigues in Europe ruled by monarchs. Voltaire tells us that at the first representation of the greatest of all plays based on the tale, the *Esther* of Racine (1688), the courtiers recognized in Esther Mme. de Maintenon, who at the time ruled the heart of Louis

XIV. Vashti was the abandoned mistress de Montespan, Haman was identified with the cruel minister Louvois, and the Hebrews prefigured the persecuted Huguenots. Voltaire was probably carried away by his sympathy for the victims of persecutions. It is rather probable that for Racine and his public the Jansenists (a Catholic movement of spiritualized religion which after 1679 was ill-treated by Louis XIV) were the people to be saved from Haman, while many verses of the drama allude to the war of Louis XIV against the Protestant coalition. The following year, the Huguenots reprinted the play in Neufchatel. For them Louis XIV was the Ahasuerus who had just (1685) expelled the Protestants from France.[50]

Thus, Esther and her Scroll continued to be admired without reservations. Hans Sachs (1494–1576), an ardent Lutheran, says that Esther represents "the righteousness in everything." Jean Desmarets (1595–1670), a Catholic poet, speaks of "the sweetness of Esther's saintly vengeance." Some writers even took Haman as the symbol of the Jews, Vashti as the Synagogue, and Esther as the Gentiles.[51]

In fact, the Protestants no less than the Catholics continued to treat Esther as a part of the divine revelation. The objections to such estimation were purely formal and easily disposed of: God is not mentioned in the Book, it contains no messianic references to Jesus Christ, and it is not quoted in the New Testament.[52]

The Enlightenment changed this mental attitude. Tolerance became the motto of the age, and the use of biblical figures by Christian sects to justify their internecine hate appeared abhorrent to followers of Locke and Bolingbroke. For instance in his *Saul* (1763) Voltaire made the king say to Samuel who demands the execution

of Agag, the captured king of the Amalekites (I Sam. 15):
"I thought that goodness was the first attribute of the
Supreme Being." Similarly, in his letter to D'Alembert
of June 15, 1768, Voltaire speaks of "the execrable cruelty
of the sweet Esther." Writing in a civilized age, he finds
grotesque the idea that a royal minister can order the
extermination of a whole people among his master's
subjects. Other Deists share his feelings. For Thomas
Paine, Esther is a "fabulous" story, though excellently
written. The atheist Sylvan Maréchal (1750–1803) naturally finds chapter 9, the Jews' slaughter of their enemies,
disgusting ("the Jews here show themselves as the true
people of the vengeful God"), but he approves the edict
by which Ahasuerus (in the Latin Bible) revokes Haman's
order, and chapter 6, Mordecai's triumph over Haman,
is for him "the masterpiece of this political novel." [53]
But on the whole English and French Deists paid no
particular attention to the Book of Esther.

The theologians of the German *Aufklärung* discovered that Esther was a document of specifically
Jewish intolerance and hatred for the human race. J. D.
Michaelis (1717–91), the leading biblical scholar of his
age, in his German translation of Esther (1783), marshaled
historical and moral objections to the book. The present-
mindedness of the *Aufklärung* induces this excellent
Orientalist to criticize the book according to the standard
of his own age. Ahasuerus in drunkenness orders Vashti
to appear before his guests. How could he, when he became sober, punish her? "Every man in our time would
have approved her refusal to come." Haman is a villain
who deserved his end, but why was he put to death without a regular trial? Michaelis reproaches Mordecai's
haughtiness before Haman, who was a royal minister,
and Esther's "insatiable vindictiveness." He reads in Esther

(8:15) that the city of Susa rejoiced at the appointment of Mordecai. "Among us it would surely be no joy were a Jew to be appointed as a Prime Minister."

Though he knows and says that the Jews, after the appointment of Mordecai, attacked their enemies in self-defense, he compares their action with the massacre of St. Bartholomew, and adds that the worst enemy of the Jews could not have invented anything more damaging to their hopes for better treatment. As these words show, Michaelis speaks in the spirit of tolerance (he mentions Moses Mendelssohn with great respect), yet the character of the German *Aufklärung* made it impossible for him and his fellow theologians to understand the Scroll of Esther.

The social and psychological structure of the *Aufklärung* compelled German theologians to find fault with the Old Testament in order to salvage their Protestant faith within the reign of Reason. For J. S. Semler (1725–91), the leader of the theologians of the *Aufklärung*, the Book of Esther exemplified the Jewish, narrow nationalist, stage in the development of Revelation. He went on to exemplify the universality of the religion of Christ by quoting gleefully a predecessor, Konrad Pelicanus (1478–1556), who had already spoken in rabid terms of the Book of Esther as describing the triumph of "perfidious" and "stinking" Jews.[54] The more the Germans became frenetic nationalists themselves, the more they condemned the particularism of the Old Testament. Throwing a public veil over Haman's decree to slay all the Jews, they condemned the Book of Esther which "breathes the spirit of revenge and haughtiness." [55]

In the meantime Germany was becoming the world center of learning. H. Taine could state in 1864: "From 1780 to 1830, Germany produced all the ideas of our historical age." The Deists' haphazard criticism was supplanted by a thoroughly reliable and systematic research in which all parts of a problem became coordinated and complementary. The Deists proclaimed that the Bible should be read "as you would read Livy or Tacitus," to quote Jefferson's letter to his nephew Peter Carr (August 10, 1787). German theologians did read the Bible as if it were non-inspired, and they did it systematically. But when they came to "the history of a personage called Jesus," to quote Jefferson again, they did not "lay aside all prejudices on both sides," but endeavored to convince themselves and their readers that, despite the biblical criticism, they could maintain their faith within the established church. Since they denied the evidential value of prophecies and miracles, they had to base their faith on the glorification of the human person of Jesus of Nazareth. Since Jesus has "to save his people from their sins" (Matt. 1:21), their humanistic theology demanded the condemnation of the Jews for their sins toward men. Hence the misunderstanding of the Scroll of Esther.

From German universities and German handbooks, the new appreciation of Esther conquered men's minds. For Abraham Geiger (1810–74), a great Jewish scholar and a courageous reformer, the Book of Esther was "of bad taste and mean feelings." Although A. P. Stanley, for instance, in his *History of the Jewish Church* (1876), still speaks of Esther in noble and understanding terms, the subsequent Germanization of theology in Great Britain and the United States made later English and American scholars parrot the German judgment. Esther is a book of "bloody vengeance" which "breathes the spirit of intense nationalism;" it expressed "a bitter hatred of foreigners," a "malignant spirit of revenge," and so on.[56]

As a matter of fact, there is no revenge in Esther. As all earlier commentators, including Michaelis, saw, the Jews did not use royal power "to inaugurate a pogrom against their enemies," nor did they carry out "against their enemies the massacre which had been planned against the Jews," [57] but, as Matthew Henry wrote, it was "their own just and necessary defense." The author of the book, naturally, has no pity for Haman, but he also tells us that Haman's order to slay the Jews "perplexed" the capital (3:15). Writing in 1908, a professor at Hartford Theological Seminary regards as improbable "that the people of Susa would feel any great grief over the destruction of the Jews." [58] This American commentator, too, copies a German book. Both De Wette and Paton proved to be good prophets but bad historians. The men of Susa, although heathens and born before the religion of love was revealed, could surely have grieved over the sufferings of innocents, even if the latter were Jews.

The Greek Esther

Lysimachus follows his original pretty closely. That, plus the influence (and imitation) of the Septuagint, gives a "biblical" coloring to his book. Yet his language is idiomatic and the Greek Esther does not read like a translation. Like every dexterous Greek writer, Lysimachus fits his style to the subject. The prayers inserted in the book sound so authentic that many students believe they were translated from Hebrew. Yet the supplications in II and III Maccabees which surely never existed in Hebrew are no less "biblical." The authors of these pieces wanted to produce precisely this impression. They could not imagine that Esther or her people in time of need would utter any but traditional prayers. On the other hand, describing Esther's dangerous going to the king, Lysimachus draws on resources of Greek rhetoric. While her face is cheerful, her heart shrinks from fear. Twice she faints during the audience. The first time, she is able to lean upon her maid, but later she falls down. Lysimachus made a particularly conscious effort at fine writing in composing two royal edicts. Here he skillfully imitates the heavy bureaucratic prose of his time, with its long sentences, use of rare words, and high moralizing tone. Haman not only bears the title of the Seleucid grand vizir; he also writes like one. It is a pity that the style and language of the Greek Esther have never been studied. The book gives a quite favorable impression of the Greek used in Jerusalem in the time of Alexander Jannaeus.

In rendering the Hebrew text, Lysimachus strives for clarity, a literary quality which was held supreme in his time. To this end he changes, omits, and adds short glosses. For instance, he inserts the name of Esther's father, which is given in the Masoretic recension in 2:15 only, as soon as the future queen is mentioned (2:7). Speaking of the conspiracy of the two eunuchs, the Hebrew says briefly but obliquely: "and the matter was investigated and found (to be so) and they were both hanged on a gallows" (2:23). Compare the Greek: "The king questioned both eunuchs and hanged them." The verse continues in Hebrew as follows: "and it was written in the book of daily records before the king." Here Lysimachus expands for the sake of lucidity, since this entry into the royal journal is of decisive importance for the plot. Thus the Greek reads: "and the king ordered to deposit for remembrance in the royal library about Mordecai's loyalty in praise of him."

Elucidation means interpretation. Lysimachus, like

all commentators after him, was at a loss to understand why Vashti refused to appear before her royal husband. But at least he had his idea why she was called: "to make her queen and put the diadem around [sc. her head]." This insertion (1:11) transforms the insolent demand of a drunken sultan into the official ceremony of *anadeixis* whereby a new queen was solemnly presented to the people. Accordingly, by means of another gloss, Lysimachus made the first feast to be the celebration of a royal marriage (1:5).

In the Hebrew Esther, the feast of Purim follows the day of victory. The day of joy is that on which the Jews found rest. But Lysimachus was used to Hellenic celebration of the anniversary day of a battle. He accordingly changed the date of slaughter. For the Hebrew author (and his rabbinic commentators) Esther's fright before Ahasuerus is normal. Lysimachus suppresses her tears and supplication when she approaches the king again after Haman's fall (8:3). And if Esther faints twice when coming to the king uncalled, she has the tact to explain it to him graciously: "I saw thee, my lord, as an angel of God." The view of a divine being, superhuman in terror or even in beauty, shakes the spectator with fright. Artaxerxes is no less courteous. He leaps from the throne to take Esther in his arms and comfort her: "I am thy brother." A ray of Hellenistic love-etiquette here penetrates into a seraglio.

Mordecai's refusal to bow down to Haman perplexed rabbinical commentators. Falling down before a superior was a common custom in the Orient. Ruth fell on her face before Boaz. But the Greeks always refused this honor to a human being, even if he was the great king. When Alexander the Great, in accordance with Persian etiquette, demanded the *proskynesis*, Callisthenes retorted that this obeisance is fit to be performed before the gods alone. Lysimachus let Mordecai say in his prayer that he refuses to bow down to any but God. In the eyes of a Jew educated in Hellenic manner, Mordecai now appeared as another Callisthenes. His insolence, heavily put on by some talmudic commentators, is here transformed into a defense of human dignity.

Mordecai's prayer is one of six completely new sections added by Lysimachus to his original. It is strange that the origin of these additions should have been questioned. The two Aramaic translations of Esther enrich the tale in the same manner with numerous insertions which surely were never a part of the original.

German theologians, who had little or no faith in Providence, pedantically discovered that the Hebrew Esther lacks the religious element because it does not expressly refer to the Lord. According to them, the translator added prayers to remedy this deficiency. In this case, however, Lysimachus would have interspersed divine names into the translated text. In point of fact, when translating, he adds references to God twice only, and in both cases to make the plot clearer: it was God who deprived the king of sleep in a fateful night (6:1); and when Haman's wife advises him not to fight Mordecai (6:13), Lysimachus adds the reason, "for the living God is with him." In the same way, Lysimachus inserted supplications to make it clear to himself and his readers not only how but also why the Jews were rescued from Haman. Esther's prayer: "Turn the heart of the king" is echoed by the words: "God changed the spirit of the king into mildness" which Lysimachus adds in the scene of the audience with the king. Esther was not the first woman who had interceded for her people before God. Judith preceded her. But in order to be heard in heaven, the intercession must be uttered by a saintly person. In her situation as the spouse of a pagan sovereign, Esther was not and could not have been an observant Jewess. To understand how, then, she could effect the rescue of the Chosen People, Lysimachus let the queen say in her prayer that she only by necessity accepted "the bed of the uncircumcised," and she remained in the faith of her fathers. The thema is prepared in 2:20 where Lysimachus construed the Hebrew text as meaning that in the seraglio Esther continued to keep the Law.

Two other additions are inserted to explain the conflict between Haman and the Jews. Since Timaeus (c. 250 B.C.E.) it had become a fashion in Greek historiography to quote documents verbatim. Authors of historical novels began to use the same literary device to set forth vital points of the story. Exercises in writing letters expressing some historical situation were part of the school program. The student, for instance, had to write a letter which Alexander the Great could have dispatched to the defeated Persian king. Inasmuch as Jewish authors who wrote in Greek necessarily passed a Greek rhetorical course, they accepted this Hellenistic fashion.

Two edicts of Artaxerxes in the Greek Esther belong to the same species, as Jerome noted. They are composed symmetrically: a blast against the Jews is answered by a counterblast against Haman. This correlation explains the divergence between the headings. The first document begins as follows: "The great king Artaxerxes . . . says thus." This is the traditional form of a Persian edict which everybody knew from Herodotus and Thucydides. The second document is couched in the form of Hellenistic "letters patent": "The great king Artaxerxes . . . greetings." The variation is intentional: writing against the Jews, the king uses the style of the Persian despot. Intervening on behalf of the Jews, he employs the polite language of Hellenistic chancelleries: "You shall do well not to give effect to the letters sent

to you by Haman." This device of variation in headings
and style was, of course, no invention of Lysimachus. A
Hellenistic rhetor, for instance, fabricated a dossier concerning Hippocrates, in which King Artaxerxes always
uses the Greek formula of salutation in his letters. But
when he is angered by Hippocrates' refusal to come to
his court, and orders him seized, the heading is changed
to the Persian style: Artaxerxes "thus says." In the first
edict, developing a hint of the Hebrew book (3:8),
Lysimachus lets the king give the reasons for the persecution. They center on Jewish exclusiveness. More or less
similar charges against Israel were made by anti-Jewish
writers contemporaneous with Lysimachus. We shall
deal with these incriminations presently. A modern commentator has suggested that these arguments put into
the mouth of Haman reveal the permanent causes of
"anti-semitism." This is not, however, the opinion of
Lysimachus himself. He rather thinks that slandering of
the Jews is a device of traitors. Artaxerxes explains this
in his second edict. Haman, a Macedonian, sought by
destruction of the Jews to transfer the Persian kingdom
to the Macedonians.

The edicts in the Greek Esther (and in III Maccabees) introduce a new feature in Jewish historiography:
the presentation of the views of both conflicting parties.
There is nothing similar in the ancient Near East. The
thundering voice of Elijah deafens us to the answer of
Jezebel. We hear the Maccabees but not their foes. A
Greek author always gave the other side a hearing. Educated in Greek rhetoric, Lysimachus works out objectively and counterposes the arguments of Haman and of
Mordecai. Both edicts of Artaxerxes are written by his
vizirs. The Targums borrowed the idea from Lysimachus
and gave an admirable summary of charges advanced
against the Jews by their detractors. It is a pity that

modern Jewish historiography has lost this Hellenic feature of presenting the Hamanic opinion objectively, exactly, and with understanding.

A third pair of additions begins and concludes the Greek Esther. The book opens with a dream of Mordecai's; it ends with Mordecai's discovery that the symbols seen in the dream announced the events narrated in the book. Mantic dreams are, of course, to be met everywhere. Like Mordecai, the Nubian king Tanutamon (663 B.C.E.) saw two serpents in a dream. His soothsayers immediately interpreted the vision as promising him dominion over the North as well as the South of Egypt. The retarded interpretation, given post-factum, of course, nullifies the prophetic value of a vision.

In Greek literature, however, it was the fashion to describe allegoric dreams, even if they remained without effect on the action. Here, the vision is only a literary method of stimulating the reader's curiosity. In the poem of Appollonius of Rhodes, Medea in a dream sees her own future in symbols. She is unable to understand their meaning. The reader, however, recognizes the fulfillment of the prophecy in the forthcoming events. In a play of Diphilus, the slave Daemones relates a dream the significance of which is hidden from him. The development of the action enlightens him and, like Mordecai, he is then able to interpret his vision.

A new episode is attached to the dream of Mordecai. He learns of a plot of two eunuchs and informs the king about it. This is an obvious doublet of the story narrated in the Hebrew book and also translated by Lysimachus (2:21–3). Why, then, two parallel stories in the Greek Esther? When an ancient author, particularly an Oriental historian, had before him two or more variants of the same story, he rarely ventured to make a choice. He rather supposed that the different versions were narrations of different events, and tried to co-ordinate the variants to the best of his knowledge and ability. Everybody knows how the same incidents are reported twice or three times in mutually exclusive parallel narratives in the historical parts of Scripture. In the Hellenistic East, Jews told various stories with considerable difference in detail about Queen Esther and the vizir Mordecai. A mural in the Synagogue at Dura-Europos shows the king and Esther together in a scene that seems to be unknown in the extant written sources. The author of the Hebrew Book of Esther collected and edited only a part of this lore. Lysimachus, however, also heard another version of the conspiracy of eunuchs. It seems that a dream led Mordecai to discover the criminal plot. Conspiracies hatched by royal eunuchs being no rare occurrence in the East, Lysimachus conjectured that his hero had saved the king twice. Accordingly, he re-arranged his sources. Following, as we have seen, a Greek literary manner, he relegated the interpretation of the dream to the end of the book. But to him the symbols of this dream hinted at the fate of the Chosen People. This interpretation thus formed a perfect conclusion to the Greek Esther and summarized its meaning. "So God remembered His people, and justified His inheritance."

Even more than Megillath Esther, Lysimachus' book is a *Te Deum* of victory. In the Hebrew work the threatened extermination of the Jews is a historical accident. We are in the world of sultans described here not less realistically than in the Arabian Nights. The despot who delivers a people to his vizir without even knowing its name is the same who has put away his wife on caprice and then executes his vizir on the word of Esther. As an ancient Jewish commentator puts it: Ahasuerus sacrificed his wife to his friend and later his friend to his wife. Haman himself plans the massacre to "save face" because a Jewish courtier has provoked him. Likewise, the spirit of revenge which German professors hypocritically blame on the book is a part of the plot. To suggest, as has been done, that Esther should have shown pity to Haman, is the same as to blame Portia for not recovering for Shylock the money lent to Antonio.

Remolding the tale, which would have charmed the jealous sultan of Scheherezade, to requirements of Greek logic and Greek rhetoric, Lysimachus unwittingly leads the Greek reader astray.

The whole Purim story hinges on Esther's keeping her origin secret. Otherwise Haman would be unable to plot against the kin of the queen. Lysimachus translated the verses stating that Esther had not disclosed her descent (2:10, 20), yet he let her say in her prayer that she had not eaten at Haman's table, nor had honored the king's feast, nor drunk the sacrificial wine. That renders the whole plot absurd. Racine has escaped the flagrant contradiction only by a subterfuge: his Esther hates the heathen feasts but does not pretend to have avoided them.

By such touches, Lysimachus changes the features of his characters. His sultana is no less pious than Alexandra, the spouse of Alexander Jannaeus. Artaxerxes is innocently deceived by Haman who attacks the Jews in pursuit of a political plan. And insolent Mordecai explains in his prayer that he is ready to kiss Haman's feet for the salvation of Israel. Note this pathetic expression of the "minority complex." The oft-quoted talmudic saying that "all Israelites are responsible for one another" refers to their responsibility before God. Mordecai speaks as a Jew of the Dispersion where the whole group is judged after the behavior of any of its members. He speaks like a metic in a Greek *polis*, who has to be in awe of the meanest of citizens.

In the Hebrew book the authorization is given to

the Jews to "stand for their life," because a royal edict, even if Haman obtained it by foul means, cannot be reversed. Taken aback by this legal paradox, Lysimachus interpreted the clause (8:3) as meaning that no man should oppose the edict on behalf of the Jews issued in the king's name by Mordecai. This new document expressly cancels Haman's orders. But now the Jewish massacre of their enemies has no justification. It becomes a pure act of revenge which punishes by death not an injury but malice. Yet it is permissible to doubt that Lysimachus was shocked by this inconsistency. By slight adjustments he has put the Purim tale into a new focus.

The meaning he gives to the story is expressed by Lysimachus himself—and twice. In Mordecai's dream and in its interpretation, the Jew as such is opposed to the Gentiles. All the nations prepared themselves to fight "the righteous nation." God had "before him two lots, one for Israel and another for the Gentiles." In a day of judgment, the Lord has chosen the lot of Israel and saved His people. The story of Purim is now another tale of the eternal conflict between "the people of God" and "all the nations."

Lysimachus must have written under the reign of Alexander Jannaeus (103–76 B.C.E.). At this date, the simple dichotomy of his book was already out of fashion. The Jews opposed to the Hasmonean king called in Demetrius III, a Seleucid, and the civil war in Judea lasted about six years. Of course Lysimachus may have been a die-hard of uncompromising nationalism. Yet, another feature of his work complicates its appreciation.

As has been said above, Lysimachus in the two edicts of Artaxerxes presents and balances pro- and anti-Jewish arguments, such as obviously were circulated in his time, about 100 B.C.E. The Hellenistic rulers (and even before them the Oriental monarchs) in their edicts used to present the reasons for their actions. Accordingly, in his persecution order Artaxerxes explains that, endeavoring to restore to his dominions peace "which is longed for by all men," he learned from Haman the cause of difficulties. A certain ill-willed people, scattered in all nations throughout the civilized world, follows laws which make it hostile to all men. For the same reason, it rejects the orders of kings, so that the stabilization of the government cannot be brought about.

Jewish exclusiveness surprised and irritated the Greeks from the beginning. Hecataeus, the first Greek author to describe the Chosen People, pointed to "something inhuman and anti-alien" in their manner of life. According to I Maccabees, Antiochus IV Epiphanes, forbidding Jewish worship, wrote "that all should be one people and that every one should give up his (peculiar) customs." The Jewish historian probably quotes from Antiochus' statement of the reasons for his edict. It is possible that Lysimachus here echoed the edict. It is surprising, however, to read Artaxerxes' deduction that the particularism makes the Jews "evil-thinking toward our state," so that, because of their machinations, the tranquillity of the kingdom cannot be attained.

In point of fact, the Jews boasted of their loyalty to their Macedonian rulers. Of course, to blacken a group you call it subversive. The Pharaoh of the Exodus had pointed to the Jewish danger. But neither he, nor, so far as I can see, his spiritual followers in antiquity, spoke of the revolutionary tendency of Israel and its laws. Caligula reproached the Alexandrian Jews for their refusal to acknowledge him as God, not for their lack of fidelity to the empire. Josephus in his treatise "Against the Greeks," refuting the prejudices against the Jews current c. 90 C.E., does not deal with the charge developed by Haman. The rabbis put a long arraignment of Israel in the mouth of Haman. The latter says that the Jews curse the king, pray that his rule may end, and avoid doing his service. But here again, as in the denunciation of the Jews (of Judea) by advisers of Antiochus VII in 134 B.C.E., the singularity of the Jews which makes them odious, makes them also isolated. They are loathsome but they do not endanger the state.

Yet, Lysimachus did not fabricate Haman's accusation from pure fancy. The roughly contemporaneous author of III Maccabees made Ptolemy IV Philopator justify his measures concerning the Jews. By reason of their particularism, the Jews are ill-willed against the king. "Thus, in order to prevent a revolution, these evil-disposed traitors must be exterminated, as befits the rebels, so that for the future our State may be settled in the stabile and best condition." The author also refers to the people who talk about Jewish worship and food laws, saying that the Jews do not share life with the king and the army, but are ill-disposed to them and very hostile to the state.

Neither Lysimachus nor the author of III Maccabees denies or belittles Jewish particularism. For them it is a self-evident truth that God has chosen Israel from among all the nations as His own people. Neither does Lysimachus appeal to the general principle of tolerance as the Jews did later before the Roman authorities. With clear reference to her later co-religionists, Lysimachus has Esther confess to God: "I hate the glory of men who break the Law." His idea is that the God of the Jews is the Ruler of the world, who gives and takes away kingdoms and empires. Thus, the heathen sovereign ought, as Artaxerxes in fact does in his second edict, to acknowledge that the Jews are children of the "Most High, Most Mighty, Living God" who guided the kingdom "for us and our ancestors," to the most perfect condition. The point of view is the same in III Maccabees and in the stories incorporated in the Book of Daniel.

This theological argument, however, acquires a new and quite secular meaning under the pen of Lysimachus. He makes Artaxerxes in the second edict turn the tables against Haman. The latter is now branded as a traitor who, by the destruction of the Jews, intended to deprive Artaxerxes of his crown "by default." The king not only permits the Jews to live according to their own laws (which are the most righteous), but also commands his subjects to aid the Jews in their defense "in the time of affliction," that is the 14th Adar. Further, Artaxerxes orders that the same day of gladness "for the Chosen People" be observed among royal holidays, as a memorial of salvation "to us and the loyal Persians" and of destruction for his enemies.

It would be difficult to push further the identification of a heathen ruler with the Jewish case. Whoever attacks the Jews is a traitor because he destroys the prop of the royal throne. Again, this political theory is not peculiar to Lysimachus. In III Maccabees, Ptolemy IV also blames the persecution of the Jews on his advisers. He asserts that their anti-Jewish suggestion was a device to deprive him of his crown and life. The Jews are his most loyal subjects and most faithful soldiers. Should one harm these "children of God," the Deity shall avenge them. The Jews, on the other hand, ask the king to deliver the apostates to them. They maintain that a man who transgresses the divine commandments cannot be faithful to the king. Accordingly, they joyfully massacre the renegades.

Thus, the Jews and their enemies, or Mordecai and Haman, say exactly the same thing about each other: the adversary is a traitor and must be punished so that the kingdom may enjoy order and peace. How is this exchange of identical indictments to be understood? Let us realize the political situation in the Levant around 100 B.C.E. From the death of Antiochus VII Sidetes in 129 B.C.E. until the end of the Seleucids in 66 B.C.E. civil dissensions ravaged Syria. Between 129 and 83 when Antioch was conquered by Tigranes of Armenia, twelve Seleucids mounted the throne; none of them reigned without a war against another pretender. In Egypt a dynastic war raged, with only short interruptions, from 132 B.C.E. until the end of the century. In this war, for the first time so far as we know the organized Jewry of Egypt entered into a coalition with a party. The Jews steadfastly supported Cleopatra II and then Cleopatra III. The origin and history of this alliance are irrelevant here. In the present state of our documentation, it is impossible to say whether other "nations" (*politeumata*) in Ptolemaic Egypt were also allied with this or other pretenders. But these groups were loose associations, and toward 100 B.C.E. the descendants of Greek immigrants in Egypt were "Corinthians" or "Macedonians" only in name. About 150 it was a man from Cos who as general of Ptolemy VI Philometor assisted Cretan visitors and Cretan mercenaries in Egypt. For this reason Jewish cohesion in the Diaspora surprised and astonished the Hellenes. Strabo notes for instance that when (some time before 103 B.C.E.) the troops of Cleopatra III went over to Ptolemy IX Soter II (Lathyros), the Jewish contingent from the military colony of Oniapolis alone remained faithful to the queen because of her Jewish generals. On the other hand, as Josephus tells us proudly, Cleopatra II entrusted her whole realm to her Jewish captains. It is also significant that though they were Oniads, that is, members of the high-priestly family dispossessed by the Maccabees, they prevented Cleopatra III from attacking Alexander Jannaeus in 102 B.C.E. by the threat that she would make all the Jews her enemies.

It is quite natural that adversaries of both queens now hurled "Hamanic" charges against the Jews. It is also probable that Ptolemy VIII Euergetes, who pitilessly punished the aristocracy of Alexandria which sided with Cleopatra II, inflicted retribution on the Jews. Writing to their co-religionists in Egypt toward the end of 124 B.C.E., the Jews of Jerusalem pray that God may "not forsake you in evil time." Some months before, Cleopatra and Ptolemy IX had patched up a peace (broken the next year), and the military success of the king in the previous years gave him the upper hand in the new coalition government. Later, in a new dynastic strife (88 B.C.E.), the mob of Alexandria, which had twice driven out Ptolemy X Alexander I, rioted also against the Jews, while Ptolemy X attacked the Alexandrians with the help of Jewish troops. At the same time (88–7) anti-Jewish disturbances occurred in Antioch. The conflict was probably related to a new outburst of dynastic strife between Philip I and Demetrius III and to the latter's intervention in the civil war in Judea. Also at the same time, in 87–6 B.C.E., Sulla sent Lucullus to restore order in Cyrene, which suffered from "continual tyrannies and wars." Lucullus had also to suppress the revolt of the Jews in Cyrene. This is the first Jewish rebellion in the Diaspora of which we have knowledge. It was, of course, a time of "unsociableness" (*amixia*), as the Greeks used to say. But let us repeat, so far as we can see the lines of separation were rather social and, as was traditional in Egypt, local. The Greek colonists in Hermonthis in September, 123, made war on Greek colonists in Crocodilopolis. In 88 as in 110 B.C.E. Pathyris held out against Ptolemy IX Soter II.

Ten years later Lysimachus' book was brought to

Alexandria. A king and queen were murdered in 80 B.C.E. The new monarch, Ptolemy XII (Auletes), was not recognized by the Romans who, as the author of I Maccabees already knew, could depose any king they wished. In Egypt, now the mob of Alexandria, now the garrison who had learnt to rule rather than obey, exiled and recalled whom they would. At this juncture, Lysimachus (as well as the author of III Maccabees) between the lines clearly suggests a road to success. Like Cleopatra III a generation before, like her mother Cleopatra II, like his uncle Ptolemy X Alexander, the monarch has to ally himself with his Jewish subjects, who are children of the King of Kingdoms and who never vacillate in their loyalty. As a second step, that would also suggest an entente, if not an alliance, with the court at Jerusalem. And then. . . .

Auletes was either unable or unwilling to follow the political line of his grandmother. We do not know whether Jewish officers in his service read Lysimachus' book. The king was expelled in 58 B.C.E. New troubles followed. In 55, Auletes bribed the Roman proconsul of Syria to restore him to the throne. The Jewish troops who guarded the entrances to the Delta opened the country to him. They acted in this way on advice of the High Priest in Jerusalem. Eight years later Caesar and Cleopatra VII, the *non humilis mulier* of Horace and Shakespeare, were besieged in the royal palace in Alexandria by the nationalist party which supported Ptolemy XIII. A relieving army marched from Syria. Jewish troops in Egypt joined the Romans. They were persuaded by Antipater (Herod's father) who commanded a Jewish contingent from Jerusalem. He referred to their common nationality and showed a letter from the High Priest Hyrcanus urging the Jews in Egypt to side with Caesar.

Modern scholars class one work as pro-Gentile and

another as anti-Gentile. With the same disarming naïveté
they can discuss whether some Greek author, say Posei-
donios, was "anti-Semitic." The Greek Esther shows that
this lazy dichotomy is not sufficient. Lysimachus firmly
believed that the Creator and Ruler of the Universe protects His Chosen People. Yet, for him, as for Ps. Aristeas
or the author of III Maccabees, there is no immanent conflict between the Chosen People and the Greeks. The
latter disapprove the persecution of Jews. Only traitors
create hostility and suspicion between the saints and their
pagan sovereign. The Jews are ready to fight for the latter, but for a price. The fact that the Jewries in the Eastern Diaspora, because of certain historical developments
toward 100 B.C.E., became separate political bodies with
bargaining power and an appetite for power explains Jewish ascendancy and also both Greek reactions to it: anti-
Jewish feelings and conversions to the Jewish faith.

NOTES TO ESTHER

1. G. Mercati, "Osservazioni a proemi del Salterio," *Studie Testi*, CXLII (1948), p. 48, n. 1. It was this observation of a Byzantine scholiast that revealed to me the composition of the Book of Esther. I alluded to it in my "Notes on the Greek Book of Esther," *Proceedings of the American Academy of Jewish Research*, XX (1951), p. 124, and lectured about it at Yale in February, 1963. In the meantime, several scholars came independently to a similar conclusion. See H. Cazelles, in *Festschrift H. Junker* (1961), pp. 17 ff., and H. Bardtke, "Das Buch Esther," in *Kommentar zum Alten Testament*, XVII, 4, 5 (1963), p. 250. We have been preceded by some playwrights of the sixteenth century who separated the Mordecai and Esther themes. See F. Rosenberg in *Festschrift A. Tobler* (1905), p. 337.

2. H. Lenzen (ed.), *XVIII Vorläuf. Bericht über die Ausgrabungen in Uruk-Warka* (1962), p. 58.

3. A. H. Krappe, *Journal of the American Oriental Society*, LXI (1941), p. 280; E. Benveniste, *Mélanges R. Dussaud* (1939), II, 249.

4. S. R. K. Glanville, *Catalogue of Demotic Papyri in the British Museum* II (1955).

5. I. Katzenellenbogen, *Das Buch Esther in der Aggada*, Diss. Würzburg (1913), p. 12. The Haggadists represented Haman as an upstart (*Megilla* 16a).

6. *La Parola del Passato* 91 (1963), p. 241. The gesture of obeisance at the Sassanian court was to prostrate oneself before the king and kiss the ground before him. Cf. W. Sundermann, *Mitteilungen des Instituts für Orientforschung* (Berlin Academy), X (1964), p. 245. Cf. J.-B. Chardin, *Voyages en Perse* (Collection 10/18), p. 59, describing the ceremonial of the royal audience: *"se mettre à genoux aux pieds du roi, à quelques pas de distance, et se prosterner trois fois la tête en terre."*

7. Cf. Plutarch *Themistocles* 13: at the battle of Salamis,

the scribes near Xerxes' seat "recorded the incidents of the battle." Cf. R. A. Bowman, *American Journal of Semitic Languages*, LVIII (1941), p. 302; Ezra 4:15; and on the royal ephemerids generally, see my observations in *Aegyptus*, XVIII (1933), pp. 350 ff. The Persian kings kept a record of their benefactors (Herodotus 8. 85), but the Book of Esther speaks of the "ephemerids."

8. Herodotus 3. 77; Plutarch *Ad Principem Ineruditum* 2.

9. N. Abbott, *Two Queens of Baghdad* (1940), p. 29.

10. Plutarch *Coniugalia praecepta* 16; *Artaxerxes* 26; Macrobius *Saturnalia* 7. 1. 3.

11. Herodotus 3. 31.

12. Abaye in *Sanhedrin* 74b. I owe the explanation of this passage to Boaz Cohen. He refers to *Baba Kama* 28b and *Niddah* 27b, where the same expression (*karke olam*) is used by Samuel.

13. *Harvard Theological Review*, LVIII (1965), p. 133.

14. Wilhelm Visher, *Das Buch Esther* (1937), p. 14.

15. On the expression *'am-'echad* (3:8) as meaning "un-important," cf. H. J. Flowers, *Expository Times*, No. 66 (1954–55), p. 273. Of course, "one" is sometimes equivalent to the indefinite article. But in our passage, *'am-'echad* explains the indifference of the king as to the massacre proposed by Haman. Ahasuerus does not care and does not need to care which is the anonymous "insignificant" people spoken of by Haman.

16. R. G. Kent, *Old Persian* (1953), p. 189.

17. al-Biruni, *The Chronology of Ancient Nations*, trans. E. Sachau (1879), p. 201. On the meaning of the word "Purim," see J. Lewy, *Hebrew Union College Annual* XIV (1939), p. 125.

18. L. Robert, *Hellenica*, VII (1949), p. 22.

19. Voltaire, *Le Siècle de Louis XIV*, ch. 27. Cf., e.g., J. G. Eichhorn, *Einleitung in das Alte Testament* (3rd ed.; 1803), II, 637.

20. M. Smith, *JAOS*, LXXXIII (1963), p. 14; Molé, *Le problème zoroastrien*, p. 27.

21. S. Lieberman, *Greek in Jewish Palestine* (1942), p. 144.

22. Cf. E. Szlechter, *Revue internationale des droits de l'antiquité*, XII (1965), p. 63.

23. Cf. J. Lewy, *HUCA*, XXV (1954), p. 169.

24. A decree of the Parliament of Paris issued on June 30, 1562, allowed everybody *prendre, tuer et massacrer* those who pillaged churches or who favored the pillards. Encouraged by this decree, the mob killed Protestants. Piguerre, *L'histoire de France*, Book VI, 12, p. 413, of the (anonymous) edition printed in 1581. According to J. W. Thompson, *The Wars of Religion in France* (1909), p. 213, the same Parliament on May 2, 1562, invited all the Catholics to organize a military league against the Huguenots.

25. *Midrash Esther, Introduction* 7, p. 2b in "Horeb" edition (1924).

26. *Megillah* 12a, 19a.

27. Herodotus 7. 169; *Scholia in Euripidem Medea*, vs. 9. 264; Aelianus *Variae Historiae* 5. 21; Plutarch *De Sera Numinum Vindicta* 557 f.

28. F. Rosenthal, *HUCA*, XVIII (1944), p. 157.

29. W. C. Lambert, *Iraq*, XXV (1963), p. 189.

30. J. G. Frazer (*The Scapegoat*, 1913) was the first, I believe, to recognize that Purim was a seasonal feast. Now cf. T. Gaster, *Purim and Hanukkah* (1960), p. 15; Gaster, *Thespis* (1961), p. 267. It does not mean, of course, that every detail of Esther's story should be explained as mirroring seasonal rites. Mordecai was no temporary "carnival" king. Demaratus of Sparta also obtained the privilege of having the Persian crown placed on his head and being led through the city in the same manner as the king (Plutarch *Themistocles* 29). When, in 1388, Richard II caused the Earl of Suffolk to sit next to him in royal robes, it provoked no little envy against Suffolk (F. R. Scott, *Speculum*, XVIII [1943], p. 84).

31. W. Henning, *Journal of the Royal Asiatic Society* (1944), p. 133; M. A. Dandamaev, *Iran Under the First Achaemenids* (1963), p. 151 (in Russian).

32. S. G. Wilson, *Persian Life and Customs* (1893), p. 201. On the duality of ancient Iranian society and the ritual combats that followed from this duality, cf. Molé, *op. cit.*, p. 15.

33. *Mishnah Middot* 1. 3. Cf. E. Unger, *Babylon* (1931), p. 81.

34. Modern commentators find here a reference to the fast on Adar 13th, which commemorates the fast ordered by Esther for the Jews of Susa before her going to the king (4:16). But the pre-Purim (or sometimes post-Purim) fast is first mentioned in post-talmudic times. H. L. Ginsberg gave me a new explanation of the passage. In 9:30, the expression "words of peace and truth" are borrowed from Zech. 8:19. The prophet promises that four days of fast shall become days of joy. The "fasts" spoken of by Esther (9:31) are these "fasts" of Zechariah (7:3, 5; 8:19). The Jews, having adopted these fasts to commemorate their misfortunes, ought now adopt the new holidays to remember their deliverance.

35. Cf. A. H. Krappe, *American Journal of Philology*, LIV (1933), p. 260.

36. Cibot in *Mémoires concernant l'histoire des Chinois*, XIV (1789). In the reign of Mahomet Khudabanda of Persia, the royal decrees were sealed by the Queen Mother (cf. Esther 9:32). H. Busse, *Untersuchungen zum islamischen Kanzleiwesen* (1959), p. 55. Cf. also V. Minorski, *Persia in* A.D. *1478–1490* (1957), p. 108.

37. J. Marquart, *Philologus*, LV (1896), p. 228.

38. *Journal of Biblical Literature*, LXIII (1944), p. 339.

39. M. Rostovtzev, *Klio*, XVI (1920), p. 203.

40. Cf. G. Le Rider, *Suse sous les Séleucides et les Parthes* (1965), p. 392.

41. Cf. G. Widengren, *Iranisch-Semitische Kulturbegegnungen in Parthischer Zeit* (1960). On Aramaic in western Iran, the use of which is attested as early as the eighth century, cf. A. Dupont-Sommer, *Iranica antiqua*, IV (1964), p. 108. In the Hellenistic period, Aramaic became a vehicle of the Zoroastrian faith (*ibid.*, p. 120).

42. J. Duchesne-Guillemin, *Le Muséon*, LXV (1953), p. 106.

43. J. Lewy, *HUCA*, XIV (1939), p. 129.

44. F. Grillparzer, in the prose outline of his drama *Esther*. *Gesammelte Schriften* (R. Backmann, ed.), III (1946), p. 149.

45. S. Jampel, *Die Beurteilung des Estherbuches*. Diss. Bern (1905), p. 5.

46. It seems that only the Abyssinian church gave Esther a place on its calendar. But the story of Esther is hopelessly confused in Ethiopic tradition. Cf. E. A. W. Budge, *The Book of Saints of the Ethiopic Church*, II (1928), p. 404.

47. *HThR*, LVIII (1965), p. 150.

48. M. Luther, *Tischreden*, Nos. 3391, 475 (Vol. XXII of the Weimar edition). Luther I, p. 5; IV, p. 499 (Weimar edition).

49. N. S. Doniach, *Purim* (1933), p. 190; J. Knox, *History of the Reformation in Scotland* (W. C. Dickenson, ed.) (1949), I, 79. The letter of Pius V is quoted in Thompson, *op. cit.*, p. 213. J. L. Motley, *The Rise of the Dutch Republic*, III, ii.

50. Voltaire, *Le Siècle de Louis XIV*, ch. 27; J. Orcibal, *La genèse d'Esther et d'Athalie* (1950), p. 21; J. Lichtenstein, *Racine poète biblique* (1934), p. 22.

51. R. Schwartz, *Esther . . . in Drama . . . des Reformationszeitalter* (1899); F. Rosenberg, *op. cit.*, p. 333; E. Forsyth, *La tragédie française de Jodelle à Corneille* (1962), pp. 169 ff., 228 ff.

52. J. G. Carpzow, *Introductio ad libros . . . Veteris Testamenti* (1731), p. 368.

53. S. Maréchal, *Pour et contre la Bible* (1803), p. 74.

54. J. S. Semler, *Apparatus ad liberam V. T. interpretationem* (1773), p. 152.

55. W. M. L. De Wette, *Introduction to . . . the Old Testament* (1843), I, 339.

56. H. Taine, *History of English Literature*, Book V, iv; A. Geiger, *Nachgelassene Schriften* (1876), I, 170; J. P.

Peters, *The Religion of the Hebrews* (1914), p. 24; H. H. Rowley, *The Growth of the Old Testament* (1950), p. 154.

57. P. Heinisch, *Theology of the Old Testament* (1955), p. 215; G. E. Wright and R. H. Fuller, *The Book of the Acts of God* (1960), p. 208.

58. L. B. Paton, *The Book of Esther* (1908), p. 297; De Wette, *op. cit.*, p. 339. On the influence of De Wette in New England, cf. S. Puknat, *Proceedings of the American Philosophical Society*, No. 102 (1958), pp. 376 ff.